INTRODUCING BEADS

INTRODUCING BEADS

Mary Seyd

B T BATSFORD LIMITED LONDON

WATSON-GUPTILL PUBLICATIONS NEW YORK

FOR ANNA, LISA AND LAURA

First published 1973
ISBN 0 7134 2439 7

Library of Congress Cataloging in Publication Data

Seyd, Mary
Introducing beads

SUMMARY   Explains processes for making beads
from a variety of materials and for using them to create
decorative and useful objects. Also presents historical
material on beads in many cultures.
Bibliography: p.
1   Beadwork–Juvenile literature.   [1   Beadwork.
2   Handicraft]   1   Title.
TT860.S49 1973 746.5 72-7393
ISBN 0–8230–6128–0

Printed in Great Britain by
William Clowes and Sons Limited Beccles Suffolk
for the Publishers
B T Batsford Limited
4 Fitzhardinge Street London W1H oAH and
Watson-Guptill Publications
One Astor Plaza,
1515 Broadway New York NY 10036

CONTENTS

ACKNOWLEDGMENT

Practically everyone I know has contributed something to this study about which so much is known and so little written. My special thanks to Barbara Williams, chief librarian at Sidney Webb College, who first noticed this; to students there, and children and teachers at Churchill Gardens and Hampden Gurney Primary School who have helped me to fill this gap.

I would also like to thank the many museum staff who have helped me, and the Craft Development Agency of Jamaica for information about tropical seeds.

Last, but not least, thanks to my husband for photography, to Con and Ena Ainsworth for checking the historical and archaeological data, and to my patient editor, Thelma M. Nye of Batsfords.

Grayshott, Hampshire 1973　　　　　　　MS

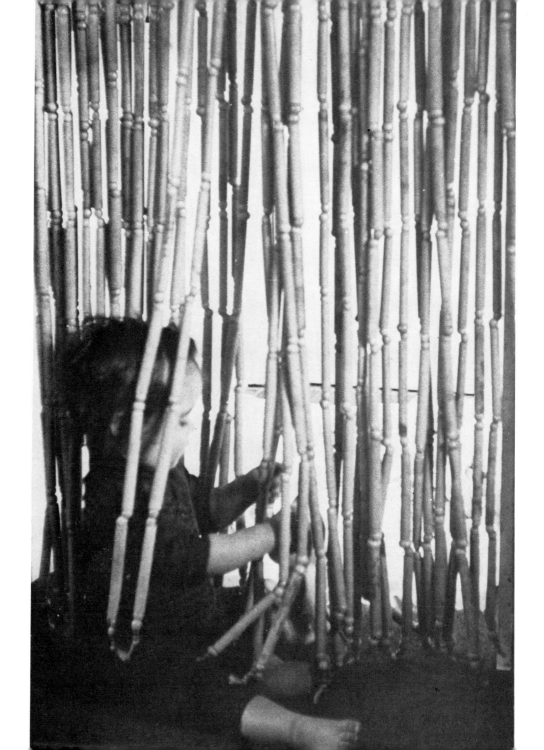

INTRODUCTION

Beads have a magical fascination . . . I once visited a school where children were busily making beads out of paper strips, and very much enjoying the activity. It struck me then there were many other ways of making beads, and what a stimulating theme this could be. Out of it would come the solutions to various technical problems and discussion on how these problems had been tackled in many parts of the world and in the distant past. The actual products could be really beautiful in themselves and could be used in many ways. I imagined groups of differing ability making beads in various ways, and one group learning from another. This could happen in a family with children of different ages, in a class with a wide ability range or in a craft centre for disabled adults – or even for very able ones. I have seen handsome ceramic beads made by craftsmen potters, and I enjoy wearing my own home-made necklaces.

So, thinking that parents and children, teachers and club-leaders might welcome a book which introduces this subject, I have tried to link the practical beginnings with facts from mythology and magic, history, geography, nature-study and very simple technology. The more one learns, the more lines of enquiry open up, so that finding out becomes a never-ending treasure hunt. Also I believe it is important that the experimental play aspect of every practical activity is kept going, ie 'There are lots of ways of doing this which could grow from this beginning' as against 'This is the way we must do it'. By our attitude we can encourage or inhibit invention. Activities which spring from using ordinary expendable materials encourage this play aspect. Once these materials were grass and clay, and they still are in the countryside. In towns and cities, waste materials are the modern equivalent, so I have included many ideas from these sources.

I have a liking for simple things. The so-called 'beggar beads' from Indian shops have always delighted me, made from seeds and pieces of twig, bamboo, porcupine quills, shells and clay. The tougher the material usually the more difficult they are to make, and so the more lasting and valuable. Making a hole in some of the hard tropical seeds is a skilled technical process, so that some of these are less easy to make than one might imagine. Even making a hole in a clay bead can pose a problem. I set myself to solve some of these problems and they led to practical experiments and to museums, antique shops and books, and to enquiries from friends all over the world.

Babies and children like to handle beads and to thread them together. They love their varied textures as well as their appearance. Many grown-ups too enjoy the feel as much as the look of necklaces and strings of beads. They are part of the playful, non-

7

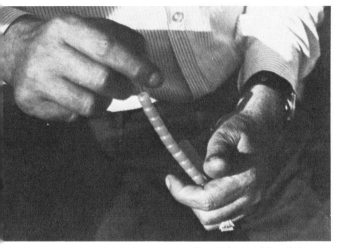

Greek 'worry' beads in use

functional 'dressing-up' aspect of dressing, as well as a demonstration of wealth. This fascination may well echo a tradition whose ritual significance is forgotten, like the blue glass good-luck beads still worn in Arab countries by children, donkeys, brides and even motorcars; as also the use of 'worry-beads' (Komboloys) in Greece, and red coral beads for children. When I was a child, it was the *normal* thing for little girls to wear coral beads, but certainly then for no superstitious reason in my case.

In the folklore of every land, coral, pearls, jewels and precious stones have been associated with magic. Intimate objects of pleasure and magical significance, beads have been despised as the poor man's jewels, and their importance has been strangely overlooked by scholars. Fearing the unknown, it is understandable that early man should use small clutchable objects – pierced teeth, shells; seed pods and 'lucky' stones – as medicines to avert sickness and amulets to work protective magic against the elements and the 'evil eye'.

In Menotti's opera, *Amahl and the Night Visitors*, King Kaspar sings about the beads in his box:
> In the first drawer I keep my magic stones;
> One cornelian against all evil and envy,
> One moonstone to make you sleep,
> One red coral to heal all your wounds,
> One lapis lazuli against quartern fever,
> One small jaspar to help you find water,
> One small topaz to soothe your eyes,
> One red ruby . . . to protect you from lightning.
> In the second drawer I keep my magic beads,
> Oh, how I love all kinds of beads!

◀ Protective charm against an evil spell, also for punishing the spellmaker *Madagascar Musée de l'Homme, Paris*

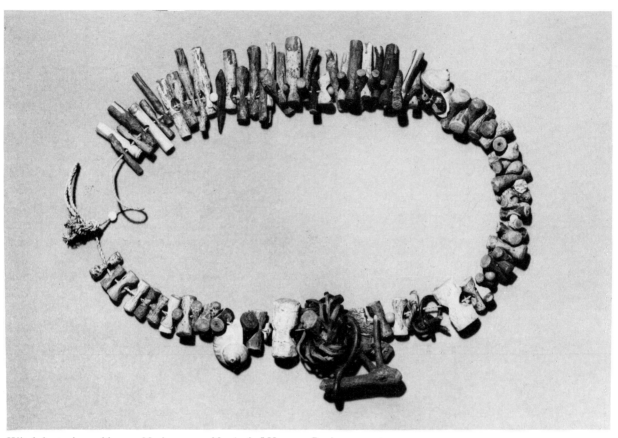

Witchdoctor's necklace   *Madagascar, Musée de l'Homme, Paris*

In her book *Bead Embroidery*, Joan Edwards refers to the use of beads as amulets, the healing properties of amber and the use of red coral by the Greeks and Romans against shipwrecks and travel mishaps. In Asia, she says, they were known to repel lightning, tempests, whirlwinds and witchcraft. In England, a string of coral beads tied quickly round the throat would stop a haemorrhage. The origin of these beliefs can be sought in the early history of amber, jade, turquoise, coral, pearls, carnelians, agates, all the semi-precious stones, and nowadays their imitations in glass and plastics.

Beads give an indication of ancient trade routes. Small and light, they are usually strung when used for trade. The abundant use of shells and shell-disc 'beads' as money in Africa, India, Polynesia, and North America until fairly recent times, suggests that certain beads have been used as coinage as far back as

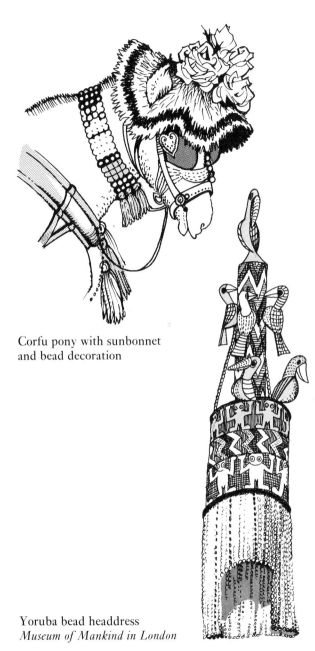

Corfu pony with sunbonnet
and bead decoration

Yoruba bead headdress
Museum of Mankind in London

the dawn of history, replacing piles of stones, knots and tally-sticks.

Commerce began with the counting and exchange of beads. In many parts of Asia the abacus, with rows of beads, is still in use in shops and markets for counting change. Variations of these are being re-introduced into schools for children learning number-work today. So important were beads to commerce that cargoes of beads from the Mediterranean and Europe were traded by explorers all over the world for ivory, animal hides, spices and precious metals, and sackfuls of trade beads were prepared for inland expeditions, whose porters and food were paid for in this currency.

A trade ship was wrecked off St Agnes in the Scilly Isles three centuries ago. After searching in the sand by Beady Pool, I was thrilled to find several tiny green glass and terra-cotta beads washed up by the sea, similar to ones I have since seen in the Museum of Mankind in London, as part of a bead head-dress.

Names given to beads throw light on their origin and function. Trade beads have been known as *conti*, *conterie* and *bugles*, sold by weight and bartered in fathoms. In contrast, the more valuable beads, for rosaries and necklaces, were *perles*, *perli* and *pearls*, sold by number. African *aggry*, *akory* or *accory* beads may well be *a coris* or *a coral*. Pearls, incidentally, have become *marguerita* in Italy, where glass beads *perli* are made, and our word *bugle* has changed its meaning now. Unravelling this tangled skein could become a study on its own.

Our English word 'bead' comes from the old Anglo Saxon *bede* meaning prayer (*biddan* to pray). Rosaries of all religions are chains of knops, knots or beads, able to be 'told' or counted in the dark. Tibetan Buddhist monks use rosaries of hard nuts and seeds, and also, in the past, of carved human bone. The rosary, connected with the rose garden in Persia, is supposed to have originated in India from the god Shiva, and to have spread east to China and Japan, and north to Tibet. Perfumed rosary beads have been made with a paste of finely chopped rose petals which becomes hard and black when dry; also with nutmegs coffee beans, cloves, tiny oranges and pomanders. These scented beads had an additional value in times when water for washing was scarce. Mohammedans use chains with ninety-nine beads to count the attributes of Allah. Buddhists, Hindus, Mohammedans and Christians alike all use this mnemonic aid 'to pray without ceasing'. Where the religious significance means little, people still use beads as 'fidgets' to help to concentrate their thoughts.

To find out more about beads and their history, perhaps the best beginning is to make some. How easy or how difficult is it to make beads? What ways can be devised? Some in fact are very easy indeed, although they may not last very long. Does that matter? Jewelry for a dramatic production, a fancy-dress party, or a school play need not last like a necklace for a Christmas present; so let us consider these very simple ones first, and then go on to more elaborate processes.

In temperate climates the best time of the year to begin would be autumn when it is easy to collect acorns, beechnuts, horse chestnuts (conkers), sweet chestnuts, and other nuts; also the seeds and stones out of soft fruit like apples and plums, melons and oranges.

People living in tropical climates can collect all manner of marvellous seeds, but some of these are exceedingly hard and have to be pierced before they become woody, or boiled before piercing, which will

Baobab seeds *Africa*

be explained later on. Following are suggested materials which are relatively easy for beginners to collect and pierce if necessary, and processes which involve a minimal number of tools.

SECTION 1 PRACTICAL WORK

Initially, bead making requires very few tools. With only scissors and paste, little children can make paper beads from strips of corrugated card. With a large pointed needle they can pierce pips and seeds, and thread them on a string with chopped sections of paper and plastic straws and macaroni. In this way they experience a variety of textures. They can also roll dough, clay, papier mâché and plaster, building their beads round wire or a toothpick, which can be carefully removed to make the next bead or left till the beads have hardened in the sun or on a radiator. Colour plate 2 shows beads made by seven and eight year olds in this way.

The next stage involves the use of a penknife or craftknife, small saws and simple drilling apparatus, of which there is a choice. Once again, if properly shown, young children can learn to handle these tools efficiently and safely. Adults need first to help them select materials which are not difficult, as initial success is a spur to greater effort later.

HARD BEADS FROM WOOD, BONE AND PLASTIC

Making these beads is a first experience in sawing.

Materials
6 mm to 13 mm ($\frac{1}{4}$ in. to $\frac{1}{2}$ in.) dowelling
Lengths of bamboo garden canes, green or dry

Bones from chicken, ham, rabbit, etc and big fish (cod-fish) cooked and cleaned
Freshly cut twigs with the bark still on, about 6 mm ($\frac{1}{4}$ in.) in diameter
Quills, ie base of big feathers from pheasants or geese (from farm or poulterer)
Discarded plastic pens or ball point pens

Tools
A small saw (junior hacksaw or tenon saw (back saw))
A penknife or craftknife
A home-made benchstop
Sandpaper
A drill (hand-drill or *Yankee* type)
A lump of *Plasticine* (*Plastiline*) if a vice is not available
Wood plank to protect the table or bench top.

Methods
Cutting Fresh twigs can be sawn or cut with a knife. The bark should still be greenish or it will crack off; left on it looks decorative contrasting with the wood. When cutting with a penknife or craftknife, the twig or bamboo can be neatly rolled to cut evenly all round. Pressure is exerted gradually as the groove gets deeper. Twigs can be cut straight or with a V cut, like sharpening a pencil (page 13). Eventually the narrow neck is cut through or snapped. Dowell is too hard to cut this way, and must be sawn.

Sawing   A bench-stop can very easily be made for sawing. Use about 205 mm (8 in.) of a 125 mm or 150 mm (5 in. or 6 in.) wide plank and two small pieces of batten, say 38 mm × 25 mm (1½ in. × 1 in.), screwed to it, placing one below and one above. If the latter are 25 mm (1 in.) shorter than the width of the plank, the table will be protected and the side of the sawblade supported. Sawing should not be a battle. Take it slowly and easily, gradually exerting pressure and letting the saw do the work.

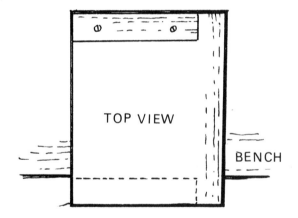

Score bark

Section 1

Section 2

Twig beads cut for drilling

Cutting green twigs

Using a saw and bench stop

TOP VIEW

BENCH

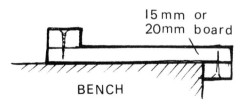

15 mm or 20mm board

BENCH

Bench stop for sawing

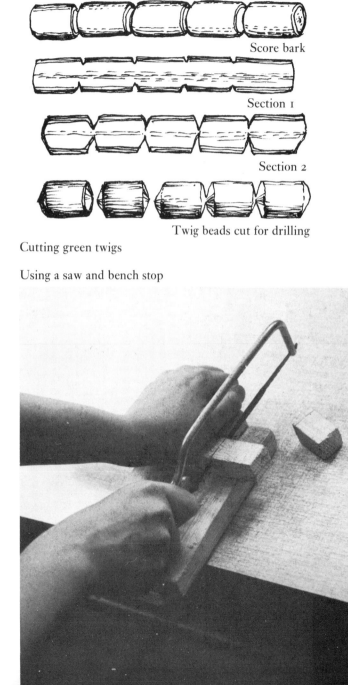

Drilling with a 'Yankee' drill

Drilling with an Archimedian drill

Drilling Bamboo, quills, bones and plastic pens need not be drilled. However, pierced *across* instead of along their length, they hang quite differently. Holes can be bored in solid wood with several kinds of drill. A drill needs a 'bit', and the size of this will depend on the diameter of the wood. A *Yankee* type ratchet drill is easy for young children to use, as is also an *Archimedian* fretwork drill, based on the same principle. These are available in hobbies shops. If a vice is not available, a lump of *Plasticine* (*Plastiline*) will hold the bead. Once the hand tools have been mastered, working with a power drill is very straightforward and easy. A brace and bit is not recommended for making beads as it is too cumbersome.

Some fishbones can be surprisingly hard to drill. They need to be wrapped in rags if a vice is used, and pierced with a fine sharp drill. A fretwork drill works well. Even an electric drill can take a few minutes.

Drilling with a hand drill

Using a bow drill

However the bones can be softened by boiling, but it is easy to make them too soft this way. Cod bones particularly present the most brilliant white, rather fearsome beads. Combined with round beads, these can be most dramatic. They can be rendered more durable by encasing in plastic embedding resin, see page 36.

Centres of bones or quills can be cleaned out with a pipe-cleaner or a needle threaded with wool.

Drilling longways and across bamboo

Finishing After cutting and drilling, these wooden beads need sandpapering well. All the wood beads (but not the plastic) can be coloured by immersing in coloured dye, dissolved in water sufficient to cover. Hot or cold water dyes can be used. The former will require simmering to obtain deep colour. After rinsing off surplus dye and drying, the beads can be sprayed with varnish or, if children are to play with them, they are best wax polished with colourless shoe or furniture cream to make them suck-proof!

The best possible covering is beeswax dissolved in turpentine by gentle heating. This must be done with care, as it could catch fire. Beeswax is exceptionally hard and can be polished up when dry. Use an old pan or an empty food can which can be thrown away afterwards, as cleaning is not easy.

Bamboo does not take dye very well, but its own colour, green or dry, makes a good contrast to dyed wood. It splinters easily when dry and needs sand-papering well.

Waxing. Immersing dyed wooden beads in turpentine and beeswax

Necklaces of bones, seeds, nuts, bamboo and wood ▶

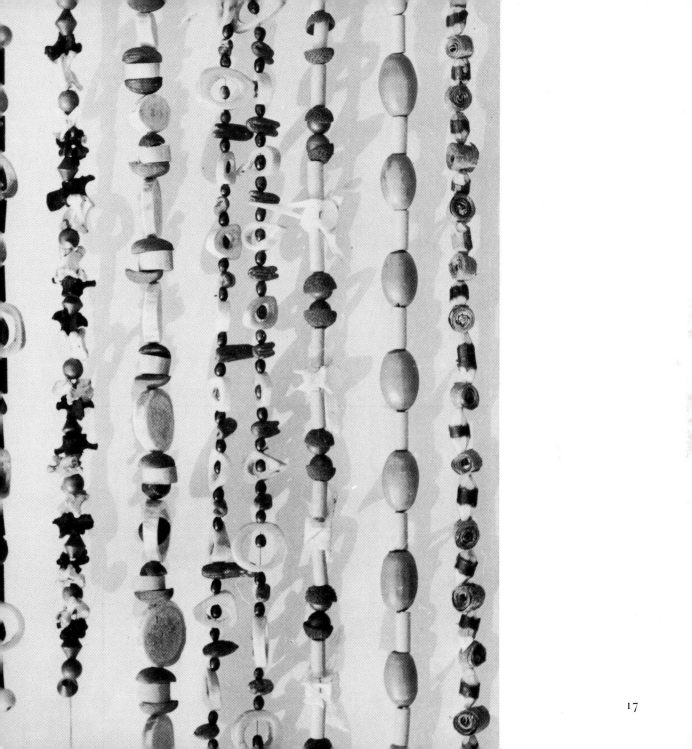

Materials
Beads can be made from most kinds of paper:
Corrugated packing paper 254 mm to 305 mm (10 in. to 12 in.) strips
Wallpaper 305 mm to 610 mm (1 ft to 2 ft)
Paper from colour magazines 305 mm to 610 mm (1 ft to 2 ft)
Cartridge, drawing, or 'cover' (coloured) paper 305 mm to 610 mm (1 ft to 2 ft)

Tools
Pencil
Ruler
Scissors
Gluestick (PVA), white glue like *Unibond* or *Elmer's*, or wallpaper paste
Brush or spreader

Method
The method of ruling out long isosceles triangles of paper which make up into beads which taper at each end is illustrated. Straight strips of paper make cylinder shaped beads.

The principle is most easily worked out with a piece of corrugated paper 305 mm (12 in.) square.

Place the corrugated paper face down onto a flat surface with the 'ribs' of the paper going from top to bottom.

Starting at the top right hand corner, mark out the right hand edge of the paper into 25 mm (1 in.) divisions.

At the top left hand corner, measure down the left edge for 13 mm ($\frac{1}{2}$ in.) and mark this measurement, then mark off the rest of this edge in 25 mm (1 in.) divisions.

Join the top left hand mark to the top right hand corner, then join the top left hand mark to the first 25 mm (inch) mark on the right hand edge. You will find that this has marked out two long triangles stretching across the paper. Join up the left hand and right hand marks in the same way until there is a series of triangles all the way down the paper. Cut these triangles out with a pair of scissors or a craft knife and a metal straight edge.

To make each bead, take a triangle of paper and fold the short, straight edge over a little way and glue using a brush with a firm PVA glue, *Elmer's* or a gluestick. It may help to fold over a matchstick or knitting needle and to use this as a roller to roll up your bead. It is necessary to glue all along the length of the triangle (except where the roller is) to keep the paper bead firm.

After practising on a big scale, try neater beads with gay sheets from colour magazines or scraps of coloured wrapping paper or wallpaper. The thinner the paper, the longer the strip will need to be, and a matchstick or knitting needle will be useful. Wallpaper paste works better with the thinner strips.

The characteristic of paper beads is the colour of the original paper. For this reason it is a pity to paint them. Experiment with other shapes – cylinders, cones, diabolos and fancy formations. Vary the widths to make long and fat beads. In Victorian England, bead curtains were made in this way and similar ones preceded the continental plastic strip *portières*, discouraging flies and yet allowing air to circulate into houses and shops from outside.

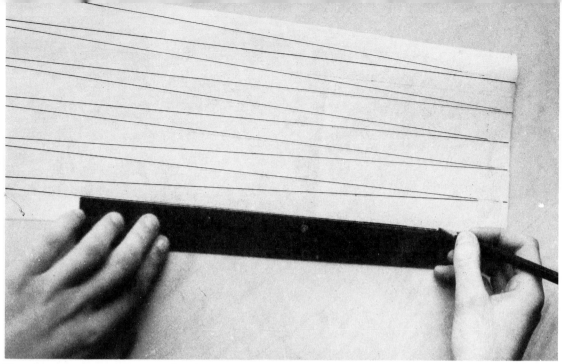

Drawing out triangles for paper beads

Cutting out the triangles with a craft knife and straight edge

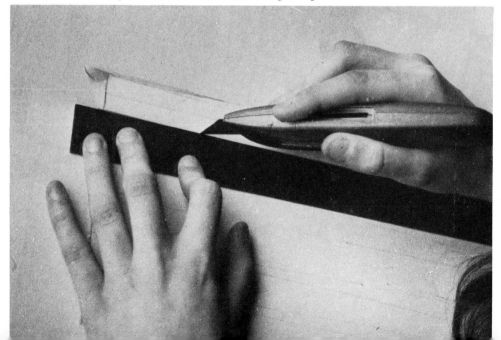

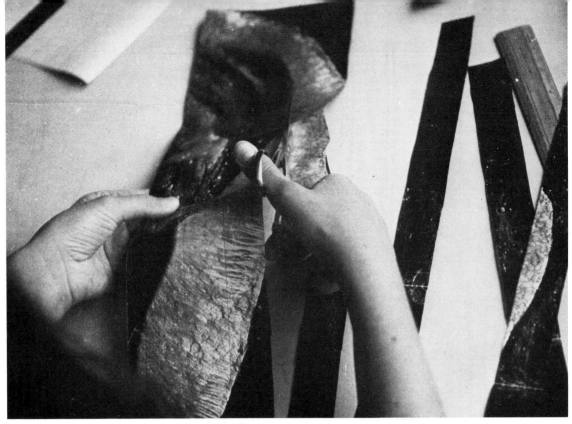

Cutting out the triangles with scissors (from illustrated colour supplement)

Pasting the triangle

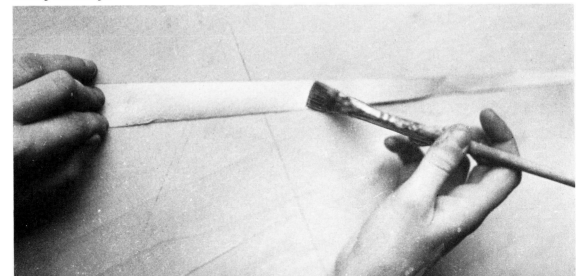

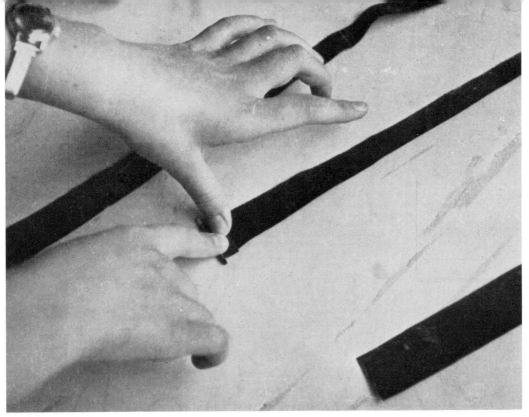

Starting to roll the triangle
Rolling the triangle

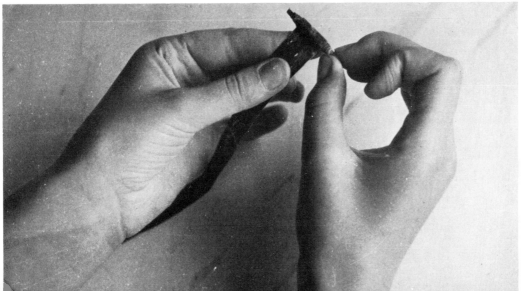

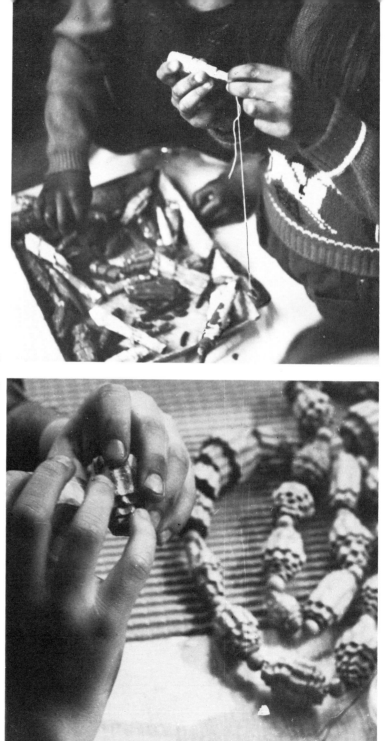

Threading paper beads

Corrugated paper beads

Papier mâché and paper beads

Children rolling clay beads

MOULDED BEADS

Here we are concerned with papier mâché, flour paste, plaster, gesso and finally with clay as materials for making beads.

Papier mâché and wallpaper paste

The are many ways of making papier mâché pulp, partly depending on what it is to be used for and who is to make it. One of the easiest ways I have discovered is to soak newspaper in warm water, dropping big sheets in whole, slightly crumpled, so that the water quickly penetrates. When the bath or bucket has as much paper as it will take conveniently, tip off the water and pull the paper to pieces, for as long as one has patience! This is a lot quicker than tearing up dry paper into little pieces, and floating them in the bucket or bath. For making small things like beads the pieces need to be smaller than for making a rough landscape or even a huge-scale mask. After soaking in warm water, it is not necessary to squeeze all the water out of the newspaper. Dry wallpaper paste is then added, which expands in the damp pulp, using up the surplus water. It is difficult to measure how much paste to paper. The best test is to mix a little, shut one's eyes and judge whether the mixture feels like damp newspaper, or more plastic and slippery like clay. The measurement is not very critical, but too little paste means that beads are difficult to model without breaking. If the mixture remains too wet, some more torn dry paper can be added in little pieces. It is not necessary to leave paper soaking all night when warm water is used. Papier mâché made with plastic paste can be stored in polythene bags, excluding air to prevent mould.

Circular beads are rolled between the palms of the hands, and with the bead lying in one hand are pricked with a metal knitting needle or bodkin through the centre. Or better, the bead can be lifted onto the needle and moulded into shape while still on it. Sometimes it helps to stick the needle into a potato or a lump of *Plasticine* (*Plastiline*) or clay, so as to work with two hands. It also helps to model around the needle particularly if the mixture is still a bit lumpy. If the bead is too sticky, french chalk or talcum powder can be used to coat the hands or whatever implement is chosen to tap the bead into shape – lengths of wood or the blade of a knife. It is not easy to do elaborate patterns on small papier mâché beads, but on big ones, for theatrical purposes, twists of string or paper tissue can be added and the whole bound with thin paper tissues, well pushed into the surface of the bead.

When the beads are dry, they shrink and crinkle quite considerably. It is possible to file down or sandpaper the surfaces to make them more perfect. Then they can be painted or varnished or sprayed with silver or gold for decoration.

Flour, water and salt
Recipe for play dough　Put a cupful of flour in a bowl, add 2 tablespoons of salt, and water to make a stiff paste. This is a dough mixture suitable for infants. The salt is for stiffening and to stop too much being eaten. It also prevents the mixture going mouldy. Too much salt attracts water, so the beads never dry. They are best dried hard on the radiator or lightly baked in the oven, after shaping in much the same manner as papier mâché ones. Dough tends to be springier and swells slightly. Powder paint can be mixed in and kneaded into the dough or it can be painted on with a little water after the beads have hardened. A touch of varnish makes these stronger

and longer lasting. They would be delightful for Christmas tree decorations, and could be fixed with cocktail sticks to hang singly or combined with small wooden beads in chains, or dressed as clowns, with paper (or bottletop) hats. This dough can be used in different coloured layers, rolled and sliced to make marbled beads.

Gesso beads
Gesso beads have been made for many centuries, a combination of whiting and glue or size, often strengthened with fibres of cotton or strands of cotton wool. Our modern equivalent is plaster of paris. This sets very quickly. For modelling by hand a slower setting plaster like *Polyfilla* is best substituted. Paste powder added to plaster of paris has the effect of slowing the setting time. Strands of absorbent cotton can be added to the mixture for strength. These beads can be modelled in a similar way to papier mâché beads or can be pressed into greased moulds to reproduce identical beads. The addition of powder colour also slows the setting time and colours the beads right through.

Clay

The same method of modelling applies to clay but of course, to be durable, clay beads need to be fired. Because the material is so plastic, and because there are so many different kinds of clay, the variety and possible subtlety of clay beads is far greater. They can be textured and decorated far more intricately than the other hand moulded types. They can be pressed into plaster of paris moulds, impressed with textures and built out with added detail. Various coloured clays can be combined on one bead.

Although clays which set hard without firing are now available, the true nature of clay is expressed in its dramatic chemical change during the process of firing and heating red hot. There is no educational value in using substitute clays, as plaster and papier mâché can be used if firing is impossible, and these have qualities of their own. For those who have gardens, sawdust firing is most successful for small things like beads. A primitive hole-in-the-ground kiln similar to the ones used by our neolithic ancestors to fire their clay cooking pots can be made on waste land or in a patch of ground using sawdust from a timber mill or the butchers. Alternatively an old metal dustbin or garbage can, with holes pierced near the bottom, can be used when it is not possible to dig a hole, or a few circles of bricks like an incinerator can take sufficient sawdust to get red hot. When children are firing kilns, obviously every possible fire precaution should be taken to prevent accidents, and the children responsible should help to take these precautions so that they are fully aware of the dangers. For some this must obviously be a holiday activity. Beads are so small that they can even be fired indoors in an open wood fire. I put mine in warm ashes on a bronze shovel, and embedding them in ashes, pushed it well

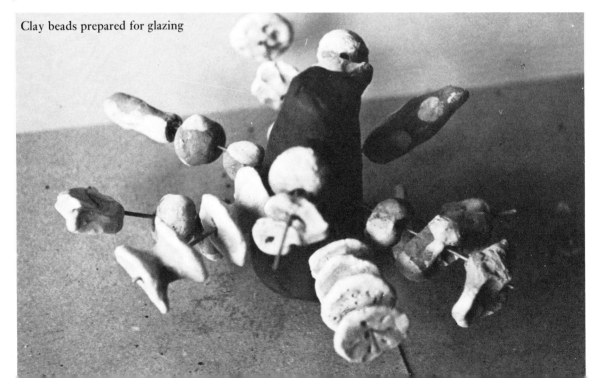

Clay beads prepared for glazing

26

into the centre of the fire, piling on more sticks and logs to get a hot blaze. In twenty minutes I pulled out the shovel with tongs and let the beads cool. I tested them in water to see if they would dissolve, but they were fired.

A further development is to make a clay collar in one piece, and then to cut it into several pieces and pierce through laterally. Alternatively, some pieces can be removed and replaced with chains of beads, the remaining pieces acting as spacers like the amber necklace in Devizes Museum, and the Bronze Age jet necklace from Argyll in the British Museum. See page 73.

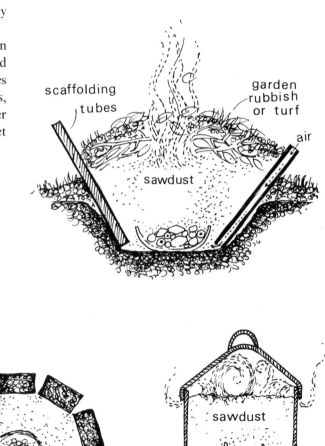

Simple kilns

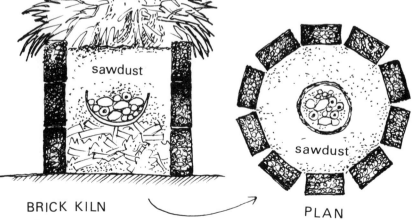

BRICK KILN   PLAN   DUSTBIN KILN

Clay beads

28

Children's necklaces from waste materials ▶

BEADS FROM BOTTLE TOPS, MANUFACTURED
PRODUCTS, PLASTIC PENS, ETC.

This type of bead is almost ready-made. It simply
requires drilling or sawing before it is ready to use.
The most obvious way to drill is not always the most
effective; how and where the hole should be drilled
depends on how the bead is to be used.

Identical toothpaste tube caps could be gay spacer-
beads used with other home-made beads. A single
one can hang like a pendant in the centre of a necklace.

Quite large plastic lids can be effective in theatrical
necklaces or combined with bamboo or corrugated
paper beads in a bead curtain. Equally, these gay but
clumsy plastic objects could be used in Christmas
decorations or mobiles, adding just the right amount
of colour and weight, like bells. Little children can
cut up plastic milk straws with scissors, and combine
them with seeds or macaroni in chains.

Silver or gold milk bottle tops (washed thoroughly)
can be crumpled into lumps or folded for decorations
or dress-up beads, or used to cover conkers or acorns.

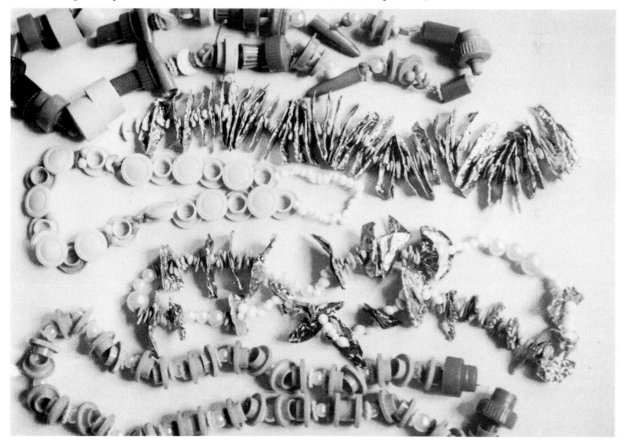

Children making pebble and thong necklaces

Seed belt *Guatamala*

SHELLS, PEBBLES AND FISHBONES

Tiny shells can be pricked with a needle, stronger ones need patience and a sharp drill, and must be held firmly in *Plasticine* (*Plastiline*) while drilling takes place. It is very important to drill in the same place in each identical shell, so that as they are strung together they form a rhythmic pattern according to their basic shape.

One of the most beautiful pebble necklaces I have seen got around the practically impossible problem of boring a hole. Instead, the pebbles were carefully selected to balance, and a black leather thong was stuck all around the edges of the flattish pebbles. Then between each a coil of brass wire was wound to keep the thongs from pulling off.

SEEDS AND FRUITS

Many pips and seeds from apples, melons and oranges are easy to pierce with a needle before they dry. Date stones drill very easily. Beechnuts can be pricked with care. Plum and cherry stones are woody and have to be drilled. Perhaps the greatest difficulty with these is collecting sufficient quantities. Here it is worth drying whole apple cores, and when enough have been collected, shaking out the seeds and discarding the cores. The same with melon seeds; if the seed and fibrous part are all put on newspaper and dried out, the seeds come away more easily and quickly. It may be easier for a group of people to work on such a project for a short concentrated time than one person for months.

Many seeds in temperate climates break too easily, but this can be a basis for experiment. Some can be strengthened with varnish or embedding resin.

Seed necklaces from the tropics

Children's necklaces of seeds, bamboo, bones and pebbles glued to leather thongs

Plate 1 Opposite
Magical *Eyebeads*, ancient and modern

Acorns can be soaked in vegetable oil until it replaces the water content. I found old acorns split very badly, but the dried cotyledons inside were as hard as wood and drilled well to make good beads. Acorn cups can be useful too, and Turkey acorn cups are most decorative.

Tropical seeds that are traditionally used as beads are usually pierced on picking, before they harden, or else they are easily bored by drilling. Some have to be boiled before drilling. Others, such as nickar nuts and red sandalwood beans cannot be boiled or the coat strips off. Of tropical seeds, the 6 mm ($\frac{1}{4}$ in.) *John Crow* bean (*Jequirity*) which is brilliant scarlet with a black dot at one end, is now forbidden for any use, as pierced it can be lethal poison. In South East Asia, its country of origin, it was once used for murder! Even *Cashew* has a poisonous shell, while *Castor Oil* seeds act as a laxative. So for bead making, one must exercise caution. The following table shows which seeds need to be softened by boiling and which can be pierced without:

Easily bored

Ackee (West Indian)	
Job's tears	Eucalyptus
Red sandalwood	Soap berry
Overlook or Jack bean	Cashew
Ironwood (*lignum vitae*)	Nickar nut
Horse-eye or oxeye bean	Casuarina

Need boiling first
Poinciana
Mimosa
Woman's tongue (West Indian)
Amber posoqueria (West Indian)

Unfortunately every tropical country has its own name for these seeds.

Moulds usually have to be made in halves. With a bead mould, a wire or string has to pass through lengthwise to keep the central hole open. Before making a mould, a prototype bead needs to be found or made from clay, papier mâché or plaster. This must be well greased with oil or vaseline. The illustrations show a mould being made of an acorn-cup.

Materials
Two fitting boxes or plastic lids about 38 mm (1½ in.) across, to contain the halves of the mould
Dentists' plaster (a small quantity – it sets more quickly than *polyfilla*)
A small plastic mixing-bowl and stick to stir the plaster
A cupful of water
A bead with a needle or wire through it, filling the hole (all well vaselined or oiled).

Method
Put half a cupful of water in the mixing-bowl and sprinkle in the plaster until it sticks up well above the surface of the water. Stir gently. Tip from time to time until it begins to set. Then quickly almost fill one of the lids and place the bead so that half of it sinks into the plaster. Put a wire through the bead to stop it falling in or getting the hole blocked. Leave half an hour to set hard. Pour water into the bowl at once before the surplus plaster sets solid. Do not pour the plaster down the drain or you will have plumbing problems! Sieve the water and put the bits of plaster into the rubbish bin.

Repeat the process in the other lid, nearly filling it with plaster. Grease the first half, with the bead

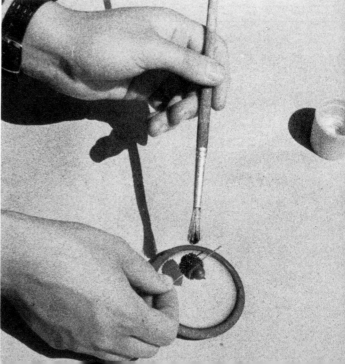

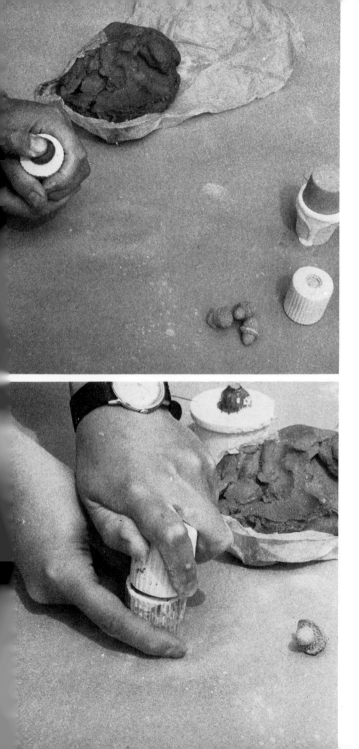

resting in it and carefully fit it over the second lid. It will be set solid but not dry. Leave the halves of the mould to dry out, with the bead between them. Mark one half of the mould 'top' and the other 'bottom', so that they can later be matched together. It is a good idea to make a small nick in the rim of the plastic so that, while the two rims are still touching, the wire or needle can yet be pulled out. Press out any surplus plaster from the lower half – you will find it best to put in slightly too much in order to get a good fit round the bead. Leave for an hour, then open up, remove bead and leave to dry overnight. When the mould is dry, vaseline it well.

Only one bead can be made at a time in one mould. When the moulds are dried out hard, a small lump of *Polyfilla* (*Speckle*) with a fine knitting needle through its centre, can be pressed between the moulds. After a short while it can be removed and surplus trimmed off round the middle. In practice, it is difficult, on this small scale, to get perfection, and sometimes better beads can be made using a single half mould and shaping the rest of the bead by hand or with a knife. I found it more enjoyable to invent faces, animals, etc, joining these beads in a necklace with simpler ones in between.

RUBBER MOULDS

Hot liquid rubber substances which set when cold, such as *Vinamould*, a hot-melt vinyl chloride, can be purchased and made up according to the instructions. They have the advantage over plaster of being springy, so that the opening can be pulled back to release the moulded bead. This saves having to make two halves. A greased stick or wire can be put into the bead substance and pulled out when it has set, leaving a hole for threading.

CEAR EMBEDDING RESIN

Hot-melt vinyl chloride is particularly suitable for use with an embedding resin, such as clear polyester resin which is poured into the mould and left to set. Sweets (candy) such as *Polo* mints (*Lifesavers*), pills, small seeds or vertebrae, can be inserted while the bead mixture is liquid. The hole can be drilled right through afterwards, or a piece of plastic covered wire can be set in and afterwards pulled out. Needles and pins do *not* pull out easily! A *very* small amount of hardener (catalyst), less than 1 per cent is needed with the resin. In making small objects it is often difficult to measure a small enough amount. However time eventually gets rid of the stickiness which ensues. One may need to wait weeks before buffing such beads.

Polo mints embedded in resin

SECTION 2 THE STORY OF ANCIENT BEADS

Crinoids
(Sea Lilies)

Ammonite

In the course of practical work we have used simple techniques and materials which are mostly very ancient in origin. History is long and complicated, but if we have a clue, something that relates events to the things we know about already, it can become like a treasure hunt. Visiting museums is much less exhausting if we go to make comparisons with familiar things. This is why I have found the study of beads an excellent introduction to ancient history. We all know something about beads. Babies clutch and cut their teeth on them; toddlers learn to thread, name and count them; school children skewer and thread up conkers (horse chestnuts); mothers know they have to be strongly strung! But few people make their own beads. After having a go ourselves, their history becomes meaningful. Looking at things made thousands of years ago is so much more interesting, after struggling to make something oneself and finding it difficult. It seems amazing that so many technical problems were solved long ago and so well – like making holes in hard stone before metal drills were invented.

In the pages that follow I have tried, as far as possible, to present facts in historical sequence, but where this has interrupted a development, I have been careful to refer to dates as well as to countries and cultures.

Beads have been made from fossils, coral and pearls, amber and most durable substances, including metals – silver, gold, copper and iron. A new field is being opened up with the development of plastics. Practically all the other technical problems were solved in antiquity, and after this families of beads can be traced back to their ancient roots. This book is an introduction to such a study.

Bellamite fossils glued onto leather

Witchdoctor's necklace *Madagascar*
Musée de l'Homme

The beginnings of beads are mingled with mystery and magic. Almost certainly the beads worn or used by men and women in pre-historic times were similar to the ones made by primitive peoples today from bones, teeth, seeds, shells, wood and clay – whatever was to hand. Only the ones made from very hard materials have survived the ravages of time. Beads certainly existed long before materials like metal and glass were worked. Amongst paleolithic, (old stone age) remains, pierced teeth and shells have been found and fossils, crinoids and ammonites, graded in size with their natural holes enlarged, giving evidence of bead manufacture at its simplest beginnings a hundred thousand years ago. According to one authority they were worn around the neck, the hips, over the ears, through the nose and even attached to eyelashes.

It is most likely that primitive people wore beads more for ritual, magic and medicines than for ornament, which explains why for thousands of years the shapes and variety have remained unchanged. Hunter-gatherer tribes still exist for us to make comparisons. In the Museum of Mankind in London there is a room depicting the Hazda tribe of Tanzania in East Africa. Here we can get some idea of the way in which human beings lived before the development of agriculture and farming. In this room are various kinds of beads, most of them worn as protections or medicines, to cure pain or keep away lions at night, or to stop children getting lost. Glass beads have been bartered from neighbouring tribes, but the rest are Hazda-made from bones, seeds, dried tubers, pods, pangolin scales, ostrich egg-shells and such like.

The earliest notable manufactured beads came from pre-dynastic Egypt. Drilling through hard materials presented a problem which was solved with the invention of the bow-drill. Alongside stone weapons and implements we find drilled beads from Baderian graves in upper Egypt. Fine examples of these grave finds can be seen in the British Museum, in the Flinders Petrie collection at University College Museum in London, and also at the Ashmolean in Oxford. The oldest go back to 4500 BC.

There are copper nugget beads, turquoise and carnelian, steatite (soapstone), alabaster and marble, ivory from the elephant and hippo, ostrich egg-shell, malachite from Nubia and shells from the Red Sea. Amongst later finds in the area are moulded beads of glass paste, and beads of quartz and steatite carved like rams and falcons, sometimes glazed blue or green with a covering called *faience*, which is practically glass and associated with bronze and copper smelting. It is produced by fusing a core of quartz crystals by heating with a little lime and oxide to colour: copper for blue, and manganese for purple and black.

Real glass appears in Egypt much later. It must have been made first by accident, by over-firing faience with too much alkaline, or as another by-product of copper-working, where spilled alkaline would form a glaze. Old glass is made by heating quartz or quartz-sand with potash or nitre, with lime, lead or copper. Faience only differs in having a small amount of alkali, and faience heated with a little surplus soda will turn to glass. Faience and glass beads were both made to imitate lapis, turquoise and carnelian, probably pierced with grass which would burn away. Faience has been called 'false

malkat', Malkat being the place in the Sinai peninsula where turquoise was first mined.

Recent research in the USSR has shown that both copper and glass were made in Georgia, near the Caucasus mountains and in the north of Mesopotamia in about 3000 BC. This is 1500 years before the glass found in Mesopotamia or Egypt. It seems likely that glass objects and glass workers were introduced into Egypt in the eighteenth dynasty (1500–1450) with the Hittite princess who married Amentophis II, in whose reign glassworks were

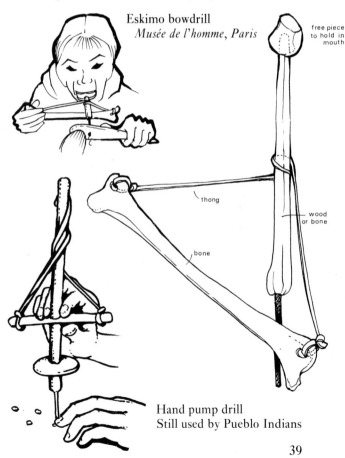

Eskimo bowdrill
Musée de l'homme, Paris

free piece to hold in mouth

thong

wood or bone

bone

Hand pump drill
Still used by Pueblo Indians

founded at Thebes and blue glass beads made at Deir el Bahri in 1400. Their son, Amentophis III who called himself Akhenaten, set up the glass bead works at Tell el Amarna. Here quantities of exquisite glass beads depicting flowers and fruit were produced, and here also some of the first eye-beads, with simple spot decoration, have been found. During this time when social organization and craftsmanship in Egypt reached its peak, there was trade with Crete and the Aegean islands, where scarabs and glass eye-beads of this period have also been excavated.

It is likely that Egyptian glass workers were exported too and set up glass manufacture in the Greek cultural centres. In Egypt delicate cylindrical beads of faience were woven into weblike covers for the mummified bodies of the pharaohs and their wives entombed under the great pyramids and in the Valley of the Kings.

Bead collar in a tomb painting, 1400 BC *Thebes*

Magical luck doll, found in a coffin,
Middle Kingdom, *c* 1900 BC *Egypt*

Badarian ୮ Faiyum "A"   c 4000 B.C   (British Museum)

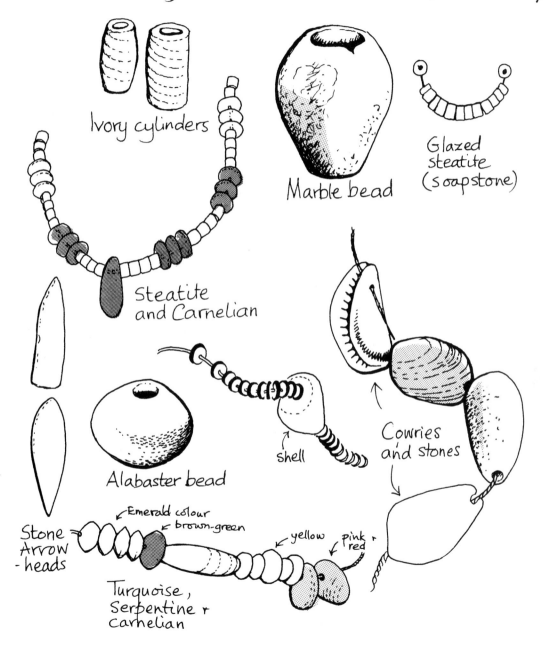

Ivory cylinders

Marble bead

Glazed
steatite
(soapstone)

Steatite
and Carnelian

Alabaster bead

shell

Cowries
and stones

Stone
Arrow
-heads

Emerald colour
brown-green

yellow

pink
red

Turquoise,
Serpentine ୮
Carnelian

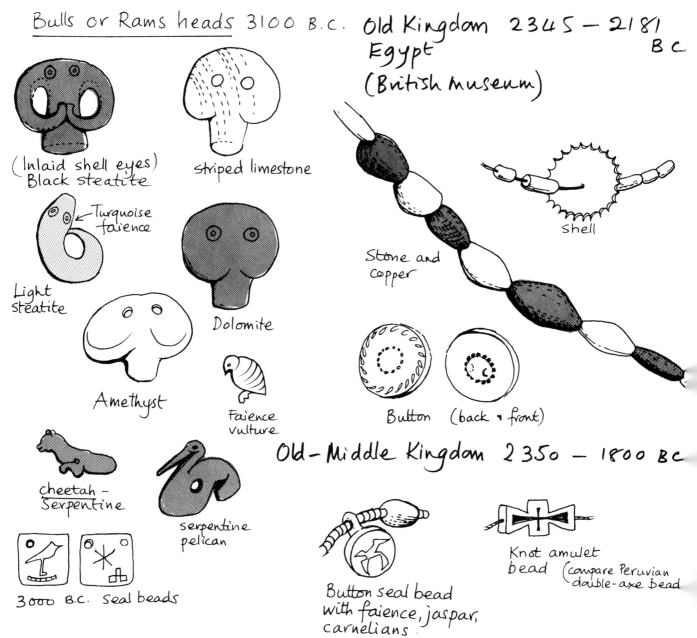

Bulls or Rams heads 3100 B.C.

Old Kingdom 2345 — 2181 B.C.
Egypt
(British Museum)

(Inlaid shell eyes)
Black steatite

striped limestone

←Turquoise faience

Light steatite

Dolomite

Amethyst

Faience vulture

Shell

Stone and copper

Button (back & front)

Old–Middle Kingdom 2350 — 1800 BC

cheetah – Serpentine

serpentine pelican

3000 B.C. Seal beads

Button seal bead with faience, jaspar, carnelians.

Knot amulet bead (compare Peruvian double-axe bead

Mostagedda –
(British museum)
c. 2000 – 1700 BC

carnelians

Faience hippo

Blue, green + purple faience

Nervita shell beads

Rock crystal →

← faience

← carnelian

Shell bead girdle

Granite

Mother-of-pearl bracelet

Faience 'crumb' beads

Pectoral and earring
from the tomb of Tutankhamun
Fourteenth century BC c 1340

43

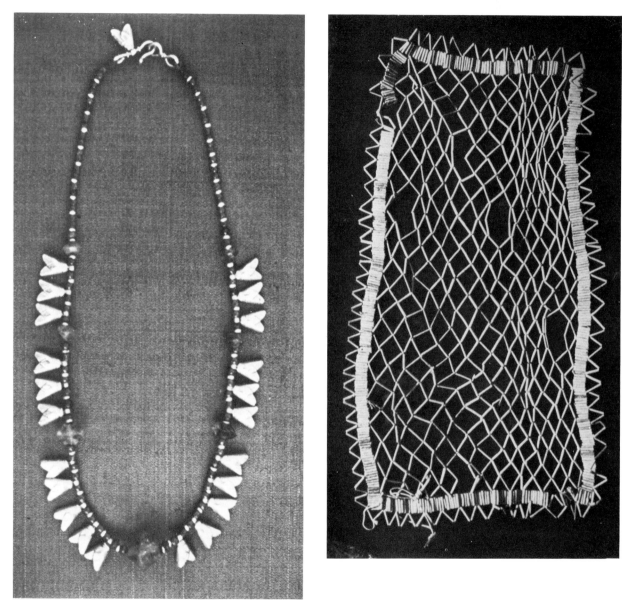

Egyptian necklace of gold bees with carnelians and amethysts

Egyptian net apron of mummy beads

A rival to Egypt's culture developed to the east in Mesopotamia. Craftsmanship and a civilization which could support it were highly advanced by 3500 BC and beads made there reflect only slightly the superb achievements during that era in building, sculpture and relief. We have evidence at Ur of a more advanced bead culture than anywhere before. A great many different kinds of beads were being worn, from ostrich egg and sea shells, lapis, carnelians and rounded pebbles to gold, pearls, carved and colourless glazed quartz and faience. Finds from Ur include red glass beads, gold beads shaped like cowrie shells and winged seeds, dating from a period of intercourse with Persia. Though there was trade with Egypt, the stronger influence came from Persia and India. From very early times, cowrie shells were used as money in the Maldive Islands, south of India, and were exported to India for very many centuries. This may have been happening as early as 1600 BC. Turquoise or malkat as already mentioned, was greatly treasured, and later mined in Nishapur in Persia, central Asia and also New Mexico, in the desert areas of the world. It became a protection for travellers and their beasts of burden, donkeys, mules and horses, making them sure-footed. The name comes from 'Turkey', and it is in Turkey that blue beads are still worn by animals, children and motor-buses!

From Mesopotamia came some of the earliest magical 'eye-beads' made from onyx, later to be copied in glass.

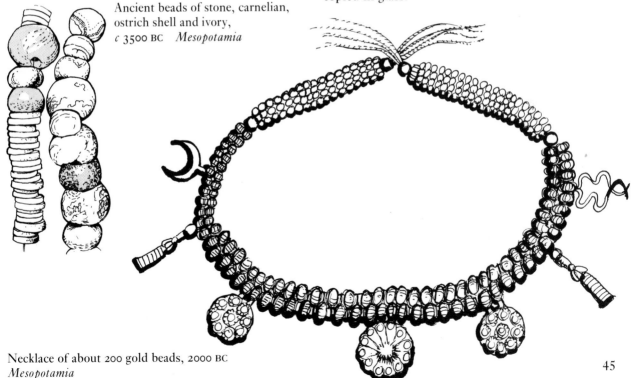

Ancient beads of stone, carnelian, ostrich shell and ivory, c 3500 BC *Mesopotamia*

Necklace of about 200 gold beads, 2000 BC *Mesopotamia*

Several centuries before glass beads were being made in Egypt, elaborate jewelry of gold and precious stones was being produced in Crete. There the Minoan civilization (connected with the worship of Minos, the Bull King) flourished for hundreds of years, its heyday being 1600 to 1300 BC. In the British Museum, there is a three-string necklace of carnelians linked with amethyst spacer-beads from Knossos which is most beautiful, and surprisingly modern looking. It is

quite different in character from the exquisite Egyptian collars and necklaces. Another Minoan necklace is of tiny green jaspar acorns, graded in size, in gold cups and setting. The palace of Knossos was destroyed by earthquake and fire about 1300 BC and Mycenaean culture from the Grecian mainland eventually dominated Crete. Very high quality jewelry, if less inventive, continued to be made, including complex gold and glass beads and pendants.

A feature of Minoan and Mycenaean gold work is granulation. This is a process whereby minute grains

Amethyst and carnelian necklace from the Aegina treasure *Crete*

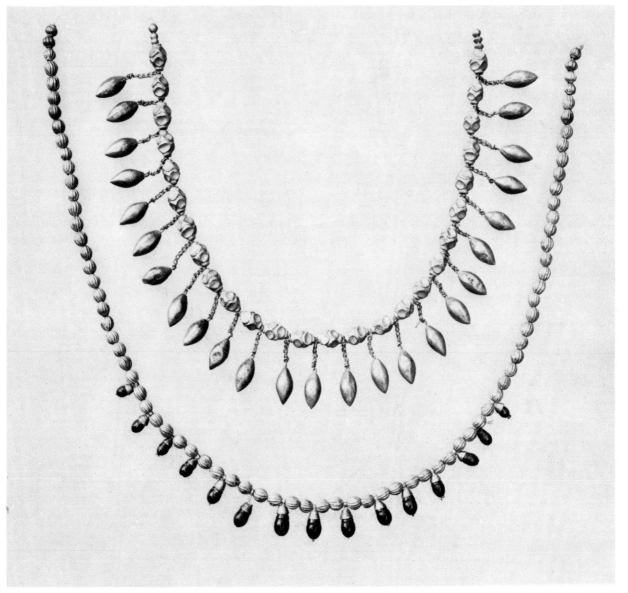

Jaspar and gold necklace from the Aegina treasure
Crete

Mycenaean gold necklace *c* 300 BC   *Enkomi*
British Museum

Granulated Minoan pendant bead *c* 1500 BC   *Cyprus*
British Museum

of gold are soldered into patterns on a background. This craft survived until Roman times, and finally the secret of attaching the grains was completely lost until just before the Second World War when it was rediscovered. Granulation was known as early as 2000 BC but was rare until 500 years later. There is a pomegranate pendant, like a huge bead, in the British Museum, which is a fine example of this art. In the Belgrade Museum I have seen others found in Yugoslavian archaeological sites.

When glass was manufactured in the Aegean, identical designs of acorns, shells, pitchers and argonauts were copied from the gold. Articulated necklaces of heart shapes and ogees are beautifully illustrated in the tomb finds of Klytemnestra. Also in the Archaeological Museum in Athens are some very ancient and beautiful glass eye-beads, Egyptian or Phoenician in origin, from Orchomenos in Heladic Troy (see page 54). Several anticipate mosaic or millefiore beads which were made later at Sidon, and later still in Alexandria.

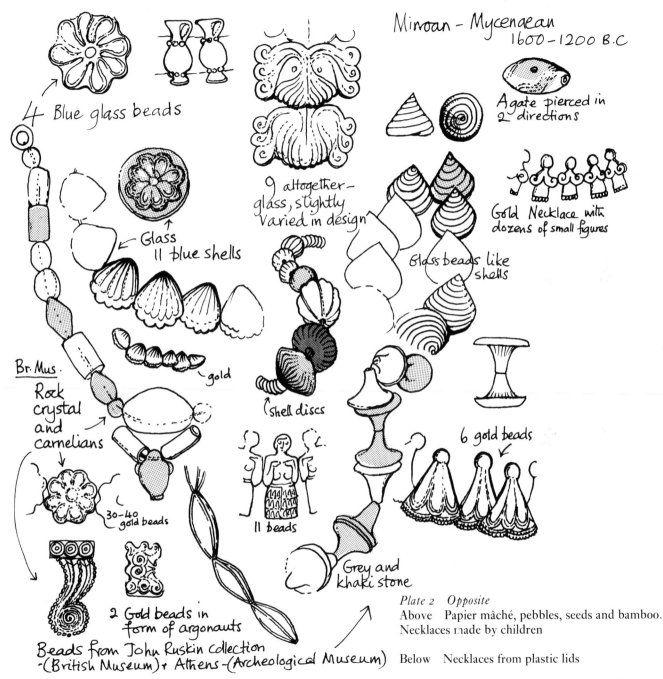

Minoan – Mycenaean 1600–1200 B.C

4 Blue glass beads

Agate pierced in 2 directions

9 altogether – glass, slightly Varied in design

Gold Necklace with dozens of small figures

Glass beads like shells

Glass 11 blue shells

gold

shell discs

Br. Mus.
Rock crystal and carnelians

6 gold beads

30–40 gold beads

11 beads

Grey and khaki stone

2 Gold beads in form of argonauts

Beads from John Ruskin collection – (British Museum) + Athens – (Archeological Museum)

Plate 2   Opposite
Above   Papier mâché, pebbles, seeds and bamboo. Necklaces made by children

Below   Necklaces from plastic lids

49

The Etruscans, based in Tuscany, had a language and religion which differed from other Italian tribes. Their period of splendour, though shorter, ran parallel with the Phoenicians for 300 years. They were great craftsmen in gold and silver, ivory and bronze, and wore quantities of jewelry. It is possible that their glass beads were imported from Phoenicia. There is a delightful Etruscan gold and glass bead necklace in the British Museum, and others in the Ashmolean Museum at Oxford. They excelled in gold granulation which technically they developed far beyond the Greeks, portraying not only patterns but whole scenes in silhouette or relief.

Etruscan necklace with gold and Phoenician glass beads Seventh century BC

Who were the Phoenicians? Their ancestors, including the Old Testament Abraham and Savah from Ur in Chaldea, came from Mesopotamia. Like the wandering Bedouin of today, they lived in dark tents and carried with them all they possessed. Over a thousand years later, by 1200 BC, descendants of these semitic migrants had established themselves in Syria as flourishing merchants, craftsmen and sea-farers along the eastern coast of the Mediterranean and had become known as the Phoenicians. They manufactured textiles and purple dye and made articles of copper and bronze and also jewelry and glass.

Herodotus in 600 BC recounts how Phoenician sailors circumnavigated Africa counter-clockwise taking three years and stopping twice to plant and harvest corn en route. Later another Egyptian planned expedition in Phoenician galleys set off to colonize West Africa. Possibly the original West African millefiore glass 'aggrey' beads attributed, perhaps erroneously, to the Phoenicians, were in fact bartered on these occasions. They have been copied by traders with Africa up to the present day, so this is almost impossible to prove or disprove.

It was at Sidon that cane glass was first made, rods of heated glass being pulled out into fine canes, (50 ft to 60 ft) long. These were dipped into molten glass of another colour and sliced into small discs which were inserted into the viscous glass bead matrix. I have a necklace of early Phoenician beads containing two square black glass beads with these concentric eyespots on four facets. Millefiori mosaic beads and glass were made in Sidon in about 300 BC and soon after that in Alexandria.

Certainly Phoenician sailors during 700 BC spread trade and culture throughout the Mediterranean and parts of Africa, venturing beyond as far as Ireland and Britain, for gold and Cornish tin. There are other fine examples of Phoenician beads in museums in London, Cyprus, Carthage, Ibiza, Athens and Samos, and in the USA.

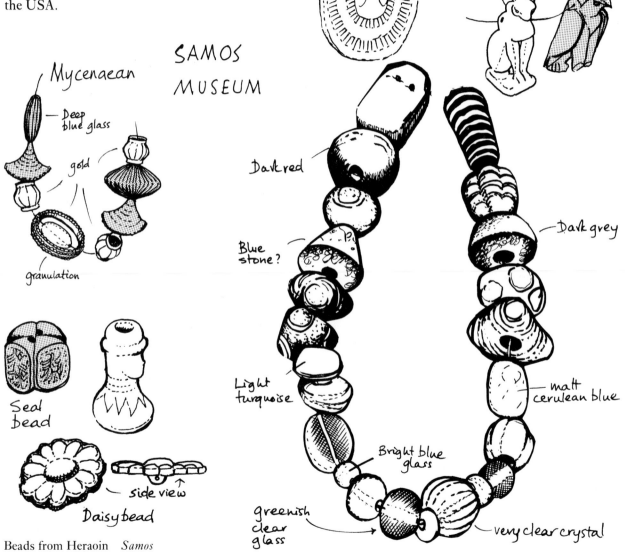

Pendant beads of Egyptian origin

SAMOS MUSEUM

Mycenaean

— Deep blue glass

gold

granulation

Dark red

Blue stone?

Light turquoise

Bright blue glass

greenish clear glass

Dark grey

matt cerulean blue

very clear crystal

Seal bead

Daisy bead

side view

Beads from Heraoin *Samos*

51

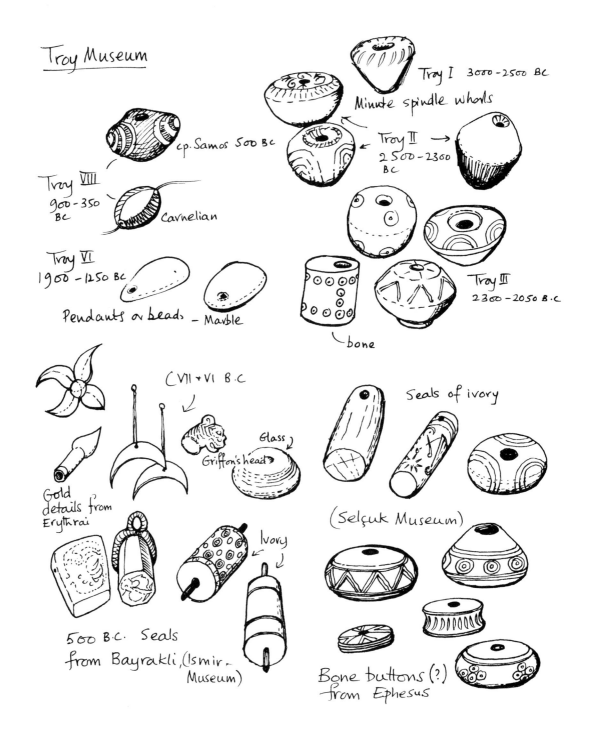

Troy Museum

Troy I 3000-2500 BC

Minute spindle whorls

cp. Samos 500 BC

Troy II 2500-2300 BC

Troy VIII
900-350
BC

Carnelian

Troy VI
1900-1250 BC

Pendants or beads — Marble

Troy III
2300-2050 B.C

bone

(VII + VI B.C

Glass

Griffon's head

Seals of ivory

Gold
details from
Erythrai

(Selçuk Museum)

Ivory

500 B.C. Seals
from Bayrakli, (Ismir.
Museum)

Bone buttons (?)
from Ephesus

MAINLAND GREECE (HELLENIC) GREEK DARK AGES AND REVIVAL PERIOD 100 TO 600 BC ARCHAIC AND CLASSIC 600 TO 330 BC

Power in Egypt gradually diminished as Phoenicia and Greece in turn became new centres of civilization. There had been cultural exchanges between Egypt and the Greek islands from very early times. Minoan and Mycenaean civilizations (2000 BC) had traded with Egypt from the second millenium when, at Epirus near Athens, crude eye-beads of glass were made in an Eye-Goddess cult which may have had its origin in Egypt or Africa. The Phoenicians later developed these more skilfully. For a while commerce was interrupted while pirates and barbarians overthrew the older civilizations, but by the eighth century BC power in Greece was growing again and Greek sailors began to challenge Phoenician supremacy at sea, Greek trade being aided by the Lydian invention of money coinage. However, this trade was restricted to the Mediterranean, the Aegean and the Black Sea, while the Phoenicians ventured further afield.

In the British Museum are wonderful examples of the Greek jeweller's art. The necklaces have pendant beads of gold and glass depicting fruit, flowers, coils and geometrical shapes. Mosaic glass (already mentioned) has been found in Greek burials, but earlier finds are most certainly from Egypt, and later ones probably from Sidon or Alexandria, which both became centres of skilful glass bead making, continuing under Roman domination. Compared with

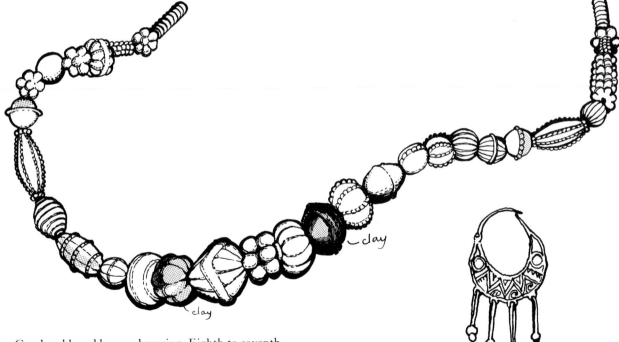

Greek gold necklace and earring. Eighth to seventh century BC *British Museum*

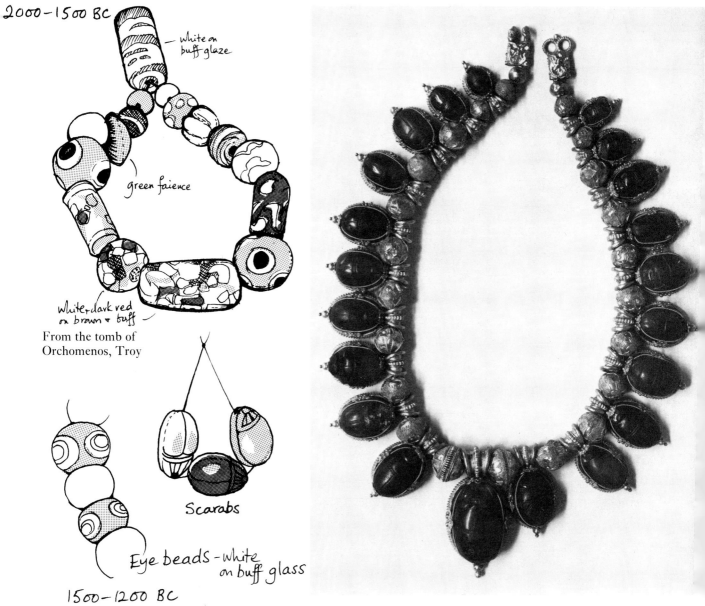

2000–1500 BC

— white on buff glaze

green faience

white dark red on brown + buff

From the tomb of Orchomenos, Troy

Scarabs

Eye beads – white on buff glass

1500–1200 BC
Early millefiori and eye-beads

54

the delicate glass beads from Mycenaean sites, some of these later ones are huge! Amber was particularly prized by the Greeks. The famous *amber routes* linked the Aegean by mule-pack to the Baltic, most important source of this golden fossilized resin, where it was exchanged for bronze weapons. Warm to the touch, glowing from pale yellow to red-orange, it floats on the sea like bubbles of congealed sunshine, which is what early peoples believed it to be. Its Greek name was *aelektrum*, whence our word 'electricity', for amber generates static electricity when rubbed. This mystic property made it highly valued for its life-giving sun like magic. Baltic amber comes from a species of prehistoric pine, whereas amber found in Borneo, Japan and South America comes from an ancient form of acacia resin.

5th Century B.C Greek

Ceramic or glass

◀ Carnelian scarabs in gold necklace *c* 350 BC
British Museum

Alexander the Great of Macedonia founded in 332 BC the Hellenic Greek city of Alexandria on the Nile delta, as a trading city with the East. Then under the Ptolomies, his successors, a flourishing glass industry grew up in Egypt, making beads in the same way as at Sidon. Because it is likely that glass beads were used mainly for trade purposes, the best collections of Phoenician, Alexandrian and Roman beads are no longer in the countries of their origin. They vary very much, from intricate small ones to huge melon beads, some over one inch across. Belgrade Art Museum has an impressive collection of these in transparent greenish glass. Similar beads were copied in iron – or perhaps it was the other way round. Beautiful examples of Hellenistic gold jewelry have been excavated in Central Europe, in Roumania, Yugoslavia and Hungary indicating either the extent of trading or the gradual migration of craftsmen to new centres.

In Asia and Syria the tradition continued without interruption. In places like Hebron and Aleppo, and in Turkey, glass bead making (Fatma Eyes) continues to this day, though many of the modern products are crudely made. Similarly, in Damascus, clay beads have been made until modern times, sun-dried and painted, or else fired in simple hillside kilns, strung on asbestos cut from the local rock and twisted into string.

THE ROMAN EMPIRE   27 BC TO AD 337

As the Romans grew in power they were greatly influenced by Greek craftsmanship. The wealthy Greeks and Romans wore intricate necklaces of gold, but glass beads had become the 'poor man's jewels',

55

mass-produced and used for trading purposes. There is a very decorative string of Roman glass beads in the Victoria and Albert Museum, which are clumsy compared with the fine faience cylinders of Egyptian mummy-covers and the dainty glass of Tel el Amarna.

What is particularly interesting is the further development of millefiori eye-beads during the period of Roman supremacy. The simple eye-beads of Tel el Amarna were made by dropping a spot of liquid glass onto a glass matrix of another colour when both were in a hot viscous state. Then one spot was added inside another, or a ring of glass or even a twisted coil was added to surround the original spot. In villages near Ismir (Smyrna), beads are still made in this archaic way. The Phoenicians at Sidon used the process involving dipped and cut off rods. Later they fused bundles of glass rod together and extended them, rather like sugar in figured rock or lollipops. This patterned rod was then cut off into discs which were placed on the surface of clear glass which was rolled flat for casting into bowls or shaping into jars, or they were also placed on a glass bead matrix and rolled into true millefiori beads. These were made extensively in Roman Alexandria and found their way into Africa.

Roman jewelry of quality was essentially gold and in later times the hardest stones, diamonds, sapphires, rubies and emeralds were cut and set in gold mounts. A form similar to enamelling, called *Niello* was also used, anticipating Byzantine development.

Roman beads *Victoria and Albert Museum*

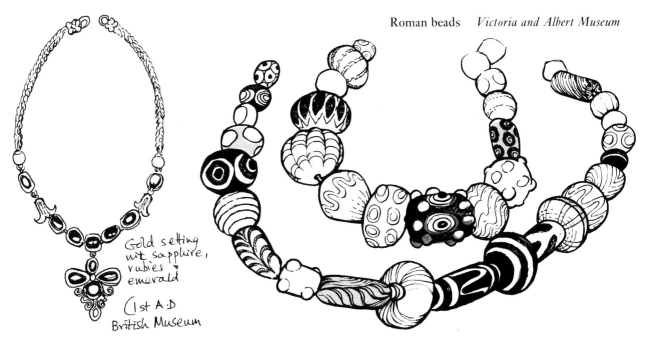

Gold setting
wit sapphire,
rubies +
emerald

(1st A.D
British Museum

Very early cameo

gold earrings

gold discs
on very
fine
gold chain

pearl

jasper
or jade

Gold + black rings

Roman jewelry first to third century AD
Belgrade Museum

After the Romans, the Arabs expanded, and their trade grew. Asia Minor was a meeting place of Greek and Persian influences. Colonized by the Hittites and later by the Greeks, then overrun by the Medes and Persians, restored by Alexander to Hellenistic Greece and later taken over by the Romans, its cities are a rich source of treasure, including many thousands of beads, cylinder seals, tiny spindle-whorls for spinning linen thread and other precious pendant objects. The illustrations show finds from Ephesus, Pergamon, Smyrna and Troy. Seals probably worn as pendants are of peculiar interest and beauty. The British Museum has a wonderful collection of these delicate pieces of craftsmanship.

The Oriental influence dominates Islamic jewelry in Asia Minor, Egypt, Morocco and North Africa, and even Byzantine Slav treasure. Pendant silver discs and crescents with bells, carnelians and coral are made up to the present day. It is interesting to trace these characteristics right back to Phoenician influences on Greek earrings of the eighth century BC, illustrated on pages 53 and 59.

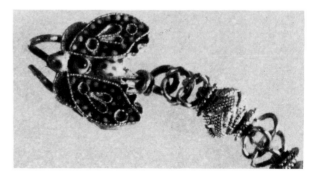

Detail of clasp on Roman necklace *c* 300 AD
British Museum

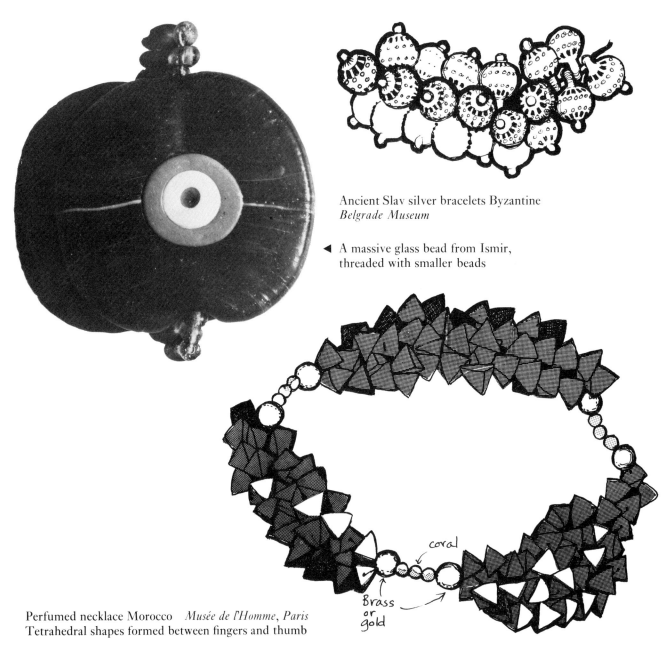

Ancient Slav silver bracelets Byzantine
Belgrade Museum

◀ A massive glass bead from Ismir,
threaded with smaller beads

coral

Brass
or
gold

Perfumed necklace Morocco   *Musée de l'Homme, Paris*
Tetrahedral shapes formed between fingers and thumb

58

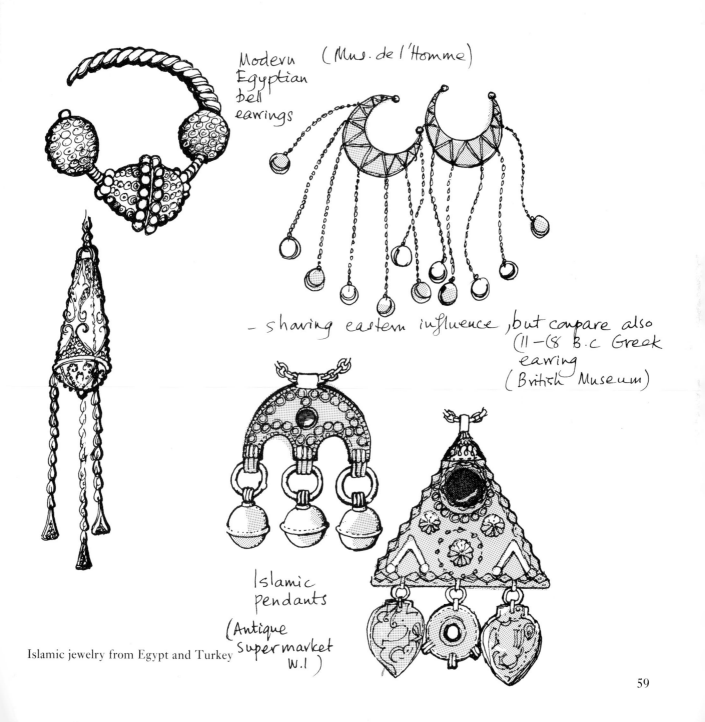

Modern Egyptian bell earrings

(Mus. de l'Homme)

- shawing eastern influence, but compare also (11–(8 B.c Greek earring (British Museum)

Islamic pendants

(Antique Supermarket W.I)

Islamic jewelry from Egypt and Turkey

Coral cap. Part of regalia of Oba of Benin
Museum of Mankind

Mosaic or millefiori beads have been traded all over Africa in particular, and throughout the centuries have been copied by glassmakers the world over as long as they continued to be valuable currency. I have seen glassmakers in Murano using the same process today.

Mrs Hingston Quiggin has a fascinating chapter on African 'aggrey' beads and legends concerning their origins. It was thought that blue coral grew in the lakes and mosaic aggry beads were some kind of seed, to be found buried in the earth. Red coral from the Balearic Isles is still used by the Oba of Benin, whose magnificent regalia can be seen in the Ethnographical section of the British Museum, the Museum of Mankind.

Very interesting research has been done into the origins of glass and other beads found in pre-European settlements in East Africa. Some date from AD 960 to 1200, including a celadon glazed ceramic bead from China (Sung period). The bulk were evidently Arab trade beads from Ptolomaic Egypt, while some were African made, in ceramic moulds, from melted down glass trade beads. This was an extravagant and clumsy process, as a new mould had to be made for each bead. These are referred to as 'garden-rollers'. It is likely that 'boiled' glass beads have been made in centres like Bieda for many centuries, using glass from bottles and trade-beads. Secrets are closely guarded and it is certain no real millefiori beads have been copied there. Nothing of modern 'civilization' has touched this ancient centre where glass is still melted in charcoal fires and hand pumped with bellows by processes which go back through the centuries. The modern products I have seen are extremely crude.

Galileo's assertion that the Earth was round, and Marco Polo's account of the wealth of the East challenged adventurers greedy for gold to seek new sea-routes to the East. In 1501 the Portuguese landed in East Africa with red beads and Cambayan cloth for barter. They discovered gold nuggets in the Zambesi and Limpopo rivers. In West Africa they found gold on the Gold (or Guinea) Coast, and Ashanti gold craftsmanship. The Musée de l'Homme in Paris has a fine collection of gold beads. They were methodically exploring for a way to India round the Cape of Good Hope while the Spaniards ventured west across the Atlantic. All carried shiploads of beads. During the years from 1500 to 1520, astronomical quantities of trade-beads were poured into Africa in exchange for gold, ivory and slaves. It was not until 1600 that the Portugese actually settled there, and the Dutch in South Africa fifty years later. By that time the Dutch were manufacturing their own cane and millefiori trade-beads at Gravelands, near Amsterdam. Two hundred years later still, Livingstone commented on the long lines of porters carrying trade-beads into Africa.

To sum up, practically all the familiar so-called 'African' glass beads came by way of trade first from the Arabs, then from Venice, and then from Amsterdam, Hamburg, Austria and Bohemia. To this day some beads are made entirely for export to Africa often to colour and patterns that have been acceptable over the centuries there, called '*African beads*' and sold to tourists as such.

Exceptions to this are the genuine coral from the Balearic Isles made into regalia for the Oba of Benin, and the clumsy striped and spotted glass beads from Bieda.

Crude African glass beads from Bieda

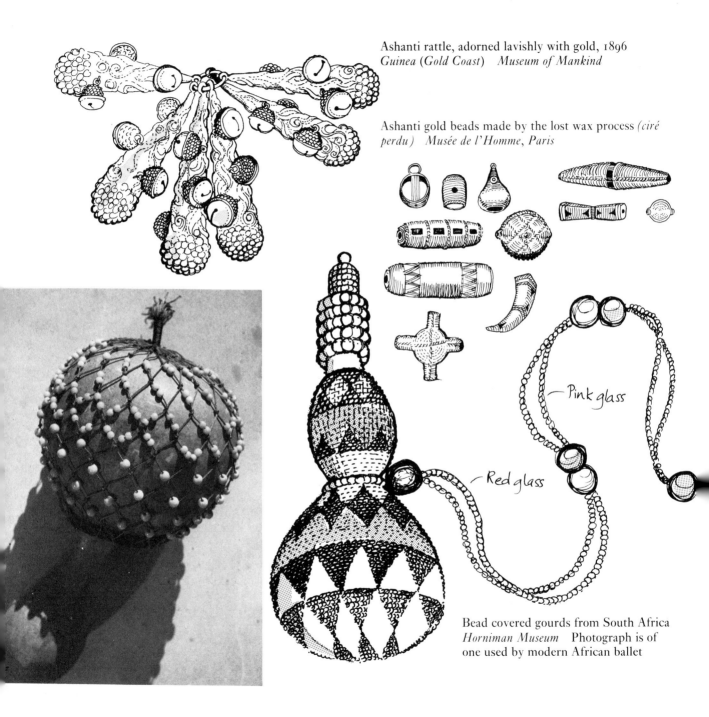

Ashanti rattle, adorned lavishly with gold, 1896
Guinea (Gold Coast)   Museum of Mankind

Ashanti gold beads made by the lost wax process *(ciré perdu)   Musée de l'Homme, Paris*

Pink glass

Red glass

Bead covered gourds from South Africa
Horniman Museum   Photograph is of
one used by modern African ballet

1863 - _Trade beads_
Blue faceted glass beads from Belgian Congo

Glass 'Aggrey' beads from Sierra Leone

Red + green on buff

Red + blue on buff

African trade beads   *Horniman Museum*

Bronze head from Benin wearing headdress of red coral beads   *Museum of Mankind*

Igbeji statuette wearing ancient glass and coral beads from Oyo   *Western Nigeria*

63

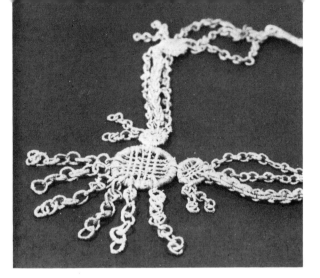

Raffia necklace from French Mauretania

Dahomey headdress *Musée de l'Homme, Paris*

Witchdoctor's necklace *Madagascar*
Musée de l'Homme, Paris

Cuffs and mask of cowrie shells *French Congo Musée de l'Homme, Paris*

Case containing Uganda king's umbilical cord, buried with his jawbone and worshipped as a god, East Africa *Horniman Museum*

65

Indian carnelians and amethysts from Cambay

We associate India with turquoise beads from Nishapur and lapis lazuli from Pamir, beads of golden grass, old-fashioned glass beads and stone beads of agate and carnelian. Some of the most interesting are etched white with the juice of the Kirar bush, drawn with a pen on the carnelian.

Indian beads of golden grass

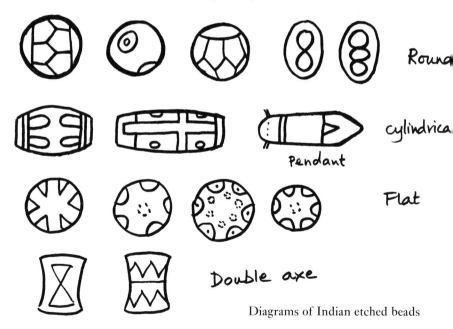

Round

cylindrical

Pendant

Flat

Double axe

Diagrams of Indian etched beads

Cambay was a very ancient bead-making centre. It is likely there was trade intercourse between the Indus Valley and India from prehistoric times. One authority claims that bead-making in Cambay has continued uninterrupted for seven thousand years. This suggests that stone and carnelian beads were being made there at the time of the Badarian culture in Egypt, before the development of civilization in either Egypt or Mesopotamia. Quantities of stone beads etched with white and black lines have been found in Indian sites dating from 2300 BC almost to the present day. In the first millenium AD, with the development of Arab trading, Cambay eventually became an important centre for trade-bead manufacture as well as textiles and continues so today.

While the Phoenicians dominated the Mediterranean and westwards, it was the Arab sailors who ventured south of the Persian Gulf to explore the Indian Ocean. After the Phoenicians, the Arabs were trading Cambayan beads for ivory and slaves to Madagascar, East Africa and Zanzibar, up the Limpopo, and visiting other parts of India, Malaya and China, right up to AD 1200, when their power was eclipsed. The Maldive Islands continued to be used as a source of cowries by the Portuguese.

Soon after this, Marco Polo, the great traveller, journeyed to the East. He describes the rosaries used by the Buddhist monks and the metal coinage of the Chinese, with a square hole in the middle, no doubt so that coins could be threaded on tally sticks or cord for safe-keeping. They also had pearls and beads of carved bone and ivory. In *The Rose Garden Game*, Eithne Wilkins makes a study of prayer beads. Patterns of religious activity, she says, are everywhere basically similar, and in all the higher religions people evoke the use of a reciter for counting invoca-

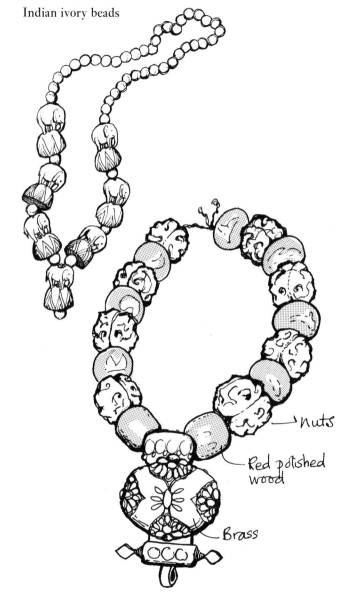

Indian ivory beads

nuts

Red polished wood

Brass

Tibetan prayer beads *Horniman Museum*

tions and for producing a state of detachment. The prayer-wheel and the rosary helped towards the approach to a spiritual centre combining, as in Yoga, mental exercise with rhythmic movement. 'Man is an animal which fidgets'. The more solitary and monotonous the mode of life, the more need to relate praying to prostration and genuflexion to combat interior chaos. So came the need to relate breathing to words and movement. St Paul's injunction to pray without ceasing (Thess 1.5.7) was helped by moving the rosary of 150 beads in three sets of five decates (this number is connected with 150 psalms). It is also associated with St Patrick and the Irish Celtic Christians; and there were 150 knights of the Round Table (*Morte d'Arthur*). In the sixth century St Columban and St Gall brought the Irish custom to the Continent, to Reichenau on Lake Constance and to St Gallen, which was later taken over by the Benedictine Order. But the Christians were some of the last to adopt the rosary. As has already been mentioned, it was originally attributed to the god Shiva in India. The Horniman Museum has an interesting collection of rosaries from Tibet and all over the world.

Jade should be mentioned in connection with both China and India. Both received their jade from Sinkiang, the mountains of Chinese Turkestan. *Seed-jade* was found in the streams, raw jade in the frozen rocks, which had to be shattered with fire. No wonder it was precious. It travelled vast distances by mule pack to Shanghai and Hong-Kong where the emperor wore tinkling pendant beads of jade. Confucius said jade contained all the qualities of excellence – nobility, purity and beauty. Jade is very hard and comes in all colours, the most famous being ranges of green. The early Chou burials (1122 BC) contained jade beads and sacred ritual symbols.

Ivory too is associated with both countries. The Chinese ivory beads are miracles of craftsmanship to this day, beautifully and precisely carved, while the Indian workmanship is freer and less perfect.

CENTRAL EUROPE

Here we must switch back again in time. During the great Mediterranean civilizations, less spectacular but none the less important developments had been taking place in central and northern Europe and its extremities Britain and Ireland. We mentioned the early development of metallurgy in the Caucasus area: the fact that glass was being made in Georgia and Azerbaijan a thousand years before the Egyptian glassworks at Thebes were begun. This knowledge of metals inevitably travelled north, east and westwards as well as south. When originally inhabited, Anatolia (now Turkey) was not the arid desert that so much of it is today. Adventurous hunter-gatherers and later nomadic herdsmen and farmers followed the fertile river valleys like the Danube into the mountains, forests and pastures of Central Europe and Asia. In Romania, fine neolithic pottery has recently been discovered, and at Boarta, gold beads and jewelry from the second millenium BC. The late Bronze Age in Romania is called the Age of Gold. Museums in Yugoslavia and Hungary also exhibit quantities of early gold, copper and iron beads as well as Greek and Roman ones from later finds. There are long strings of gold beads, some round, some conical tubes, some

◀ Tibetan prayer beads *Horniman Museum*

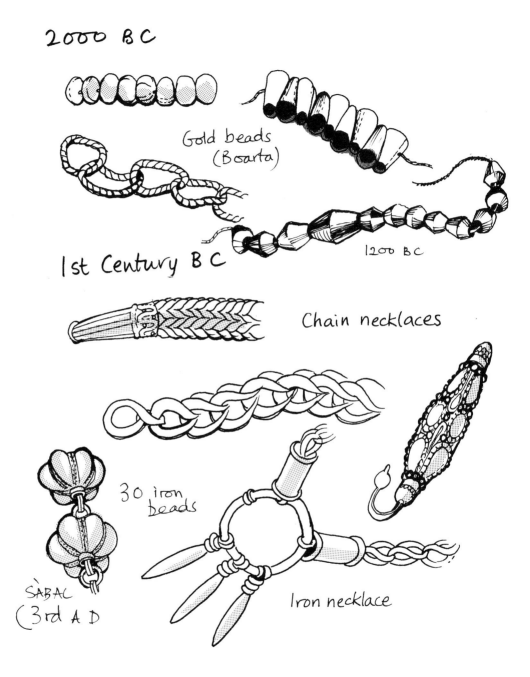

2000 BC

Gold beads
(Boarta)

1200 BC

1st Century BC

Chain necklaces

30 iron
beads

SABAL
(3rd AD

Iron necklace

like chain links. From the same area in the first century AD, came exquisitely worked Dacian iron chain belts and necklaces that resemble Greek and Mycenean emphorae and pitcher beads, and which may have been made by imported craftsmen originally. Heavy glass vessels, window panes and wonderful glass mosaics as well as glass beads were made in the second and third centuries at Garni, ancient residence of the Armenian Kings. In

Europe in the fifth century AD it seems there was a decay in glasscraft and some processes were forgotten, later to be revived in Venice. Tamurlane introduced glass craftsmen to Samarkand in Georgia, who continued to work there into the eleventh and twelfth centuries AD, and similar work was done at Krakov and Wroclav in Poland. At this time glass manufacture was being developed in Venice and Venetian craftsmen later took glass bead manufacture to all the cities of Europe, for trade purposes and for jewelry and rosaries.

In Austria the use of 'need-beads', a form of rosary or magical string of oddments, has persisted in peasant districts almost to the present.

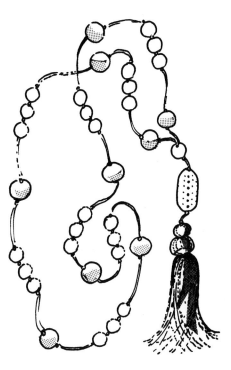

Nineteenth century Chinese necklace of ivory and blue glass beads on a silk thread

Eighteenth century Austrian 'need-beads' for protecting ▶ children from sickness and the Evil eye
Horniman Museum

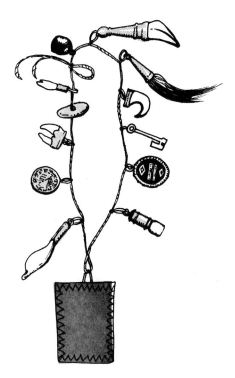

71

In paleolithic times, before the last period of glaciation and during the millenia which preceded Bronze Age metallurgy in Central Europe, *homo sapiens* had penetrated parts of Britain and Ireland as well as the rest of the Continent. W N G Van der Sleen reports finding a pierced horse tooth amongst Solutrian remains at Ceyrac in the Cevennes (France) and late paleolithic pierced wolves teeth have been found. Human remains have been found in southern England in Kents Cavern, Devon, of similar age together with remains of extinct animals. Crinoid fossils which had been used as beads have been found dating from Acheulian times, that is, long before 30 000 BC.

More important finds in our bead treasure-hunt date from the Bronze Age, beginning about 2000 BC when the 'Beaker Culture' came to Britain. Amber beads have been found in narrow graves at Aldbourne, Wiltshire, together with native faience, lignite and ecrinate beads and a pendant and objects of bronze. At Rillaton in Cornwall, where the famous gold cup was discovered, there were also beads and a bronze dagger. At Upton Lovell, Wiltshire, there were eleven cylindrical gold buttons, and at Stockbridge Down in Hampshire a necklace of calcite, jet, lignite, shell and faience (probably from Egypt). Four decorated bone beads were found in Folkton, Yorkshire, in a bowl barrow grave. The most spectacular find is from Melfort, Argyll, where a jet collar necklace with many rows of spaced beads was found with bronze armlets in a stone burial cist. Native jet is a form of hard coal found in north-east England near Whitby. The beads mentioned are all sufficiently durable to have travelled many thousands of miles, and perhaps as many years, as possessions or with traders from the places where they were originally made.

Gold beads in Wessex may have come from Ireland, where beads of amber, pierced bone and green glass as well as spiral gold wire have been found. For thousands of years traders from the Mediterranean and invaders from the Continent left their traces in Britain. Phoenicians traded for tin; Romans brought craftsmen from many countries; Britain probably learned glassmaking from Gaul; Vikings, Saxons and Danes invaded and were absorbed or repelled. First century Viking chequer beads from graves in Gotland are most elaborate affairs of mosaic glass. Anglo-Saxon beads of glass and quartz, which are also types of eye-bead and show skilful workmanship, have been found in Kent and Cambridgeshire. Possibly originals were imported and local craftsmen copied with their own variations. The Anglo-Saxon have a dull red matrix with yellow impressions or eyes, or vice versa. Before Roman times these colours were not used. Devizes Museum has a fine collection of all these early beads.

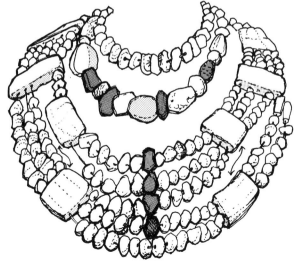

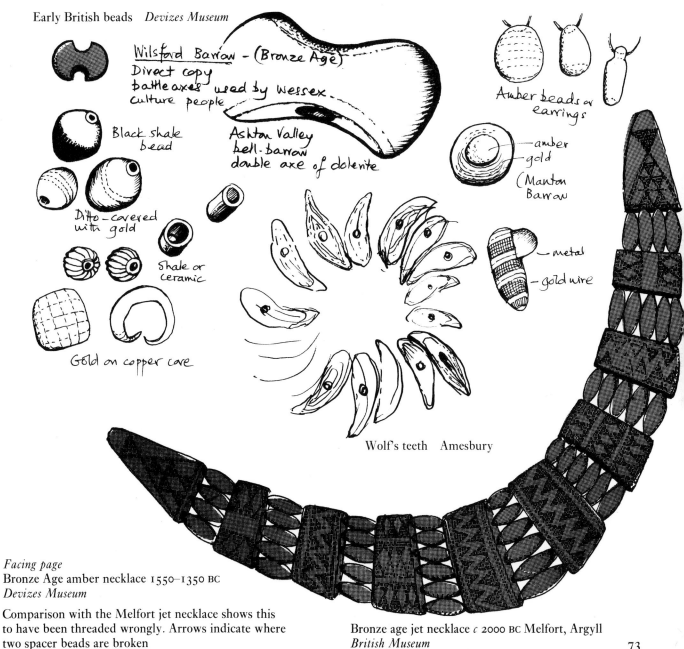

Early British beads *Devizes Museum*

Wilsford Barrow - (Bronze Age)
Direct copy
battleaxes used by Wessex
culture people

Black shale
bead

Ditto - covered
with gold

Shale or
ceramic

Gold on copper core

Ashton Valley
bell-barrow
double axe of dolerite

Amber beads or
earrings

— amber
— gold
(Manton
Barrow

— metal

— gold wire

Wolf's teeth   Amesbury

Facing page
Bronze Age amber necklace 1550–1350 BC
Devizes Museum

Comparison with the Melfort jet necklace shows this
to have been threaded wrongly. Arrows indicate where
two spacer beads are broken

Bronze age jet necklace *c* 2000 BC Melfort, Argyll
British Museum

The rivers of Russia yielded quantities of pearls from freshwater mussels, and from medieval times onwards religious icons and costumes – particularly women's caps – were richly adorned with pearls. When sewing pearls to large pieces of work, one woman would sit under the table while another worked from the top. At times when the church was poor, beads took the place of gems. Similarly, in Germany beads and pearls were sewn onto vellum for illustrations like small-scale mosaics, as in the Byzantine bible-cover illustrated. Pearls are associated with the moon. They are formed by the oyster secreting nacre over a tiny speck of grit, and they can go on growing for twenty years. Man learned to culture pearls by inserting some small irritative object inside the shell, and pearl fishers would examine and collect them, their lungs bursting for

Byzantine pearl-decorated bible cover *Biblioteca Marciana, Venice*

Illuminated page depicting pearls and gems MS Douce 219 folio 40 *Bodleian Library, Oxford*

air, in waters often infested with sharks. No wonder they were short-lived! The small pearls from fresh water are called *seed-pearls*. In all their soft iridescent colours, and when fresh not too difficult to pierce, they are surely nature's most perfect bead.

VENICE

At the time when Arab trading was diminishing, Venice was developing as a centre of trade and wealth. Glassmaking there dates back to the eleventh century AD. Marco Polo was a Venetian, born in about 1254. He told of the wealth and high civilization in India, China and Japan and described the fine porcelain and craftsmanship in precious metals and carved ivory. The Venetian glassmakers studied antique glass and perfected crystal and spun glass. They made goblets decorated by the millefiori technique as well as copying Phoenician and Roman beads. In 1291 the glass ovens were taken to the island of Murano and the secrets closely guarded. In spite of this, however, Venetian craftsmen escaped to Attar in Spain and were lured to the growing cities of Europe, including London where a Venetian, Jacob Verzalli, was granted a monopoly for making Venetian glass. An industry was established in AD 1570 at Crutched Friars in East London. In Bohemia, centred round Gablonz, Venetian beads were imitated. These eventually dominated world markets, right up to the present day. In the glass museum at Murano I have seen exquisite filigree white glass beads of the sixteenth century, and among the modern glass beads being made there are some which are sophisticated and charming too. The tiny glass beads are called *seed* beads. The colour was originally sucked up narrow tubes by mouth before dividing it into beads. Now it is done by a chemical process – the secrets still carefully guarded.

Opaque white glass beads *c* 1600 AD
Murano Glass Museum, Venice

Precolumbian Mexican sculpture

In AD 1517 when Spanish explorers first sighted Mayan stone buildings on the mainland of Mexico, at Catoche, Bernal Diaz describes how men in ten large canoes put out towards their anchored ships and came aboard. They were cheerful and friendly and a string of green glass beads was given to each man. In the days that followed an enormous amount of gold was bartered for green beads which the Mayans thought were jaspar, not knowing how to make glass. They prized jade and jaspar more highly than gold. Clay figurines from Mexico's ancient civilizations show modelled collars and necklaces of beads. They made necklaces of carnelian, gold and shells. In the Anthropological Museum in Mexico City I made a drawing of an Aztec necklace of carved beads in the form of skulls. The Diego Rivera collection there also contains particularly choice examples of necklaces and figures with huge beads, and so does the Musée de l'Homme in Paris.

Similarly, ancient Peruvian beads were made of stone, carnelian, amber, gold and turquoise, some of the latter curiously carved like double axes. This bead from ancient Peru shows striking similarity to one in the Egyptian collection in the British Museum, which would please Thor Heyerdahl.

Skull necklace. Post-classical Huastic culture
Anthropological Museum, Mexico City

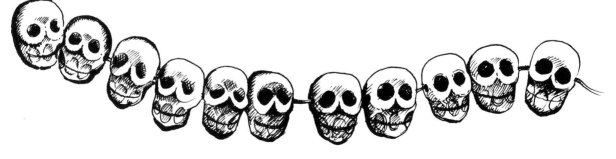

Turquoise bead - 1500 AD
from Peru, similar
to double axe design

1882   light
        blue   Opaque
                            blue
                            Turquoise
                            Glass +
                         Amber beads
                         from Ujiji
(value = 4 yds. thin calico)

Silver 'shells'
(worn on a cord)
from Borneo
 - Shan states

Pods used as rattles
 - Bolivia, S. America

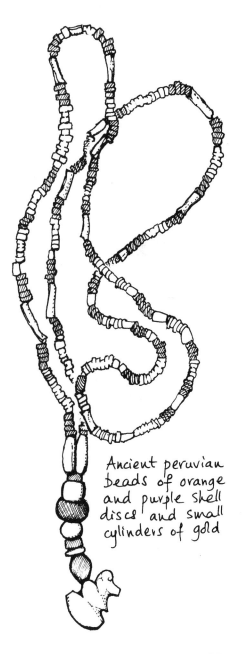

Ancient peruvian
beads of orange
and purple shell
discs and small
cylinders of gold

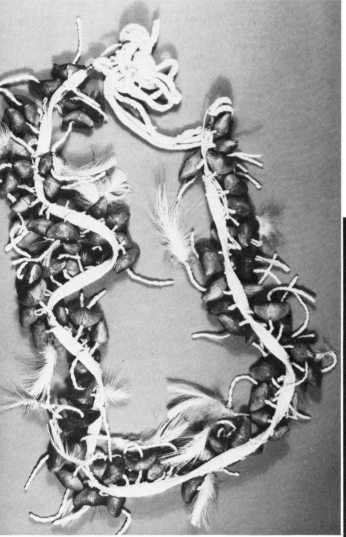

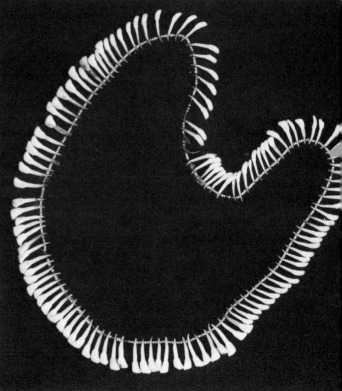

Necklace of deers' teeth, Wapisiana people, Guyana,
South America   *Horniman Museum*

Necklace of nuts and feathers. Medicine man's rattle,
Makusi people, Guyana, South America   *Horniman
Museum*

These islands were the last to be inhabited by man and the last to be explored by Europeans. The story of their beads, like those of the Red Indians, is intimately connected with the development of primitive currency. They used jadeite, coconut shell, seeds, whales' teeth and quartz pebbles. Most common were the discs of polished shell or coconut: 'Abuta' or 'Mauwai' in the Solomon Isles, measured in fathoms and spans, one fathom being six feet. In 1912, $\frac{1}{4}$ fathom, equal to a shilling (5p), would buy a small carrying net, a pot or a basket; 1 fathom would buy a good arm-ring, a large pot, a large basket of taro, a club or a spear; 10 to 12 fathoms would buy a large pig, or hire a murderer, or purchase a widow; 100 fathoms or more were necessary to atone for a murder, or buy a girl wife. 100 fathoms would be put into a netted bag and placed as a pillow for ancestral ghosts. The outraged lover sang

> If you did not want me
> Why did you tell me to give you a string of red shell money?
> Your father demanded two hundred fathoms of abuta;
> That was your price.

In the *Story of Money*, Mrs Hingston Quiggin goes into much more fascinating detail.

The Horniman Museum has an excellent display of primitive currency from all over the world. Perhaps the most beautiful and delicate is from St Matthias, where a string of iridescent blue-green beetles' legs are strung like a necklace of fine glass beads. Thor Heyerdahl mentions in *Aku-Aku*, that archeologists digging on Easter Island found a blue Venetian 'pearl' several feet down among rubble.

Rattan ball beads

Asmat – New Guinea and Borneo

– Balls or beads of rattan palm

Engraved pearl shells or phallocrypt, pendant discs from Australian aboriginal tribe

Currency beads from the Pacific Islands

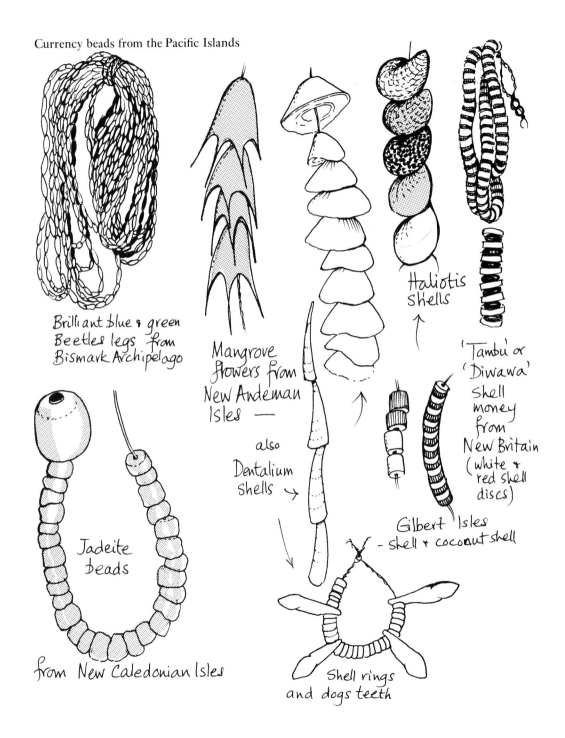

Brilliant blue & green
Beetles legs from
Bismark Archipelago

Mangrove
flowers from
New Andeman
Isles —

also
Dentalium
Shells →

Haliotis
shells

'Tambu' or
'Diwara'
shell
money
from
New Britain
(white &
red shell
discs)

Gilbert Isles
- shell & coconut shell

Jadeite
beads

from New Caledonian Isles

Shell rings
and dogs teeth

The Dutchman, Roggeveen, the first European to sail in those waters, discovered the island on Easter Day 1772. His logbook records how the first native to board his ship was presented with two strings of these blue beads and also a small mirror and a pair of scissors. I saw one of these faceted 'blue pearls' in the Peruvian exhibit in the *Musée de l' Homme* in Paris. In Fiji and Borneo decorative tourist necklaces are still made from shells, pierced seeds, and plaited and rattan palm ribs. The illustrations show how beautiful some of these arrangements can be and how varied the hard shells and seeds from tropical countries. Aboriginal beads from Australia have been made from jade and nephrite, which is similar. The famous New Zealand Maori 'Hel-tiki' magic talisman pendant is also of jade. These countries abound in semi-precious stones.

Plate 4   Opposite

Beads of seeds, shells, paper, bone, ivory and glass

Necklaces of shells and plaited palm ribs ▶

81

In Chaco Canyon, near Pueblo Bonito in New Mexico, quantities of hand-drilled turquoise beads and ear-pendants have been found originating from Colorado and Nevada, and the value of it is immortalized in the rites of the Zuni and Nevaho Indians. The northern American Indians add an important chapter to our bead history. They made bead coinage of dark and light shell, ground smooth into small cylinders like glass. Called 'wampum' this coinage was made into belts for personal adornment or prestige. A symbol of authority or power, it was surrendered on defeat in battle, and used as a visible record of transactions. On special occasions squaws wore as many as 200 strings. The loose bead coins were used as small change for silver exclusively for trading between the American Indians and the white settlers. They measured 3 to a penny, or 360 (a fathom) to 5s; except in Massachusetts where it was 4 to a penny, or a 240 fathom to 5s. By 1800, Crow Indians would pay a horse for 100 blue beads. The fathom was a length of beads wherever explorers ventured in the Pacific too. Modern North American Indians do elaborate braids, aprons and belts, using a loom and a weft threaded with tiny seed beads. The Hudson's Bay Company has beautiful examples on exhibition at Beaver Hall near Mansion House, London.

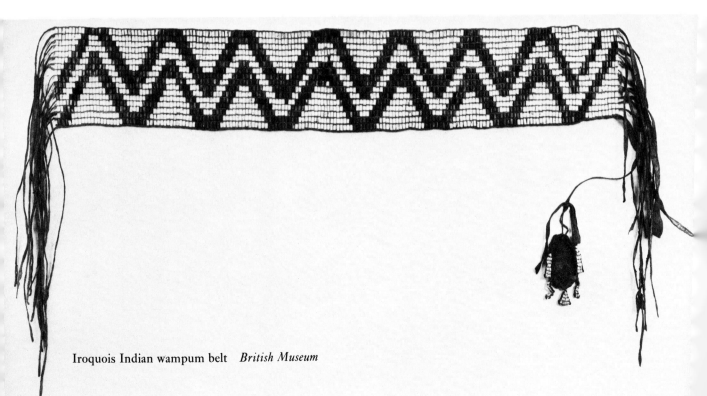

Iroquois Indian wampum belt *British Museum*

The Eskimos of the Far North are natural artists who still decorate their canoes and harpoons and carve small animal-beads from bone and stone. These are often pierced like pendants and worn singly on a thong. Trade beads of glass are worn in summer by the women, threaded into net-like capes and worn dangling from elaborate chignon bands, and men wear bead-decorated tunics and thigh boots.

Eskimo ivory seal beads

Eskimo bead chignon

From this summary it can be seen that practically all modern bead forms, barring plastics, stem from techniques discovered and perfected in antiquity. We have mentioned most of the reasons why beads have been used, and though *ornament*, adornment and display of *wealth* have played their part, we shall only find jewellers interested in the more valuable ones. The rest we could equally describe as *medicines*, *magic*, *prayer-beads* or *money*. A study of *trade* will open up the lives of explorers and ordinary people hundreds of years ago up to the present. *Jewelry* will give us a glimpse of their tribal chieftains and the lives of their aristocracy. Also through beads we would follow the development of mathematical ideas, of world religions or glimpse at geography through the names and language of beads. In order for our studies to be meaningful, we shall need to carefully select what direction to take for further study and define its limits, because the field is too vast. When art and craft is used as a service to another discipline, such as history, we must make sure the quality of the artistic, aesthetic experience is not submerged; so if we make beads as part of an integrated study, we must make sure first that we make and display them well. I have concentrated on the variety and complexity of beads around us, in and out of museums, as a stimulus to make our own and arrange them in beautiful and interesting ways. Others may give the theme completely new directions and disciplines.

In the pages which follow I have confined myself to ways in which hand-made beads can be used now. There are many publications dealing with traditional forms of beadwork and bead embroidery which are outside the scope of this book, but mentioned in the bibliography.

SECTION 3 USING HAND-MADE BEADS

Knowledge of the past can be a spur to creativity. Beads have been embroidered, woven, knotted and even knitted into fabric. In medieval times and the early Renaissance, fortunes were spent on elaborate clothes enriched with jewels and pearls. Bead embroidery came as an economic substitute for gems. In the fifteenth century in Germany coral beads were substituted for jewels on ecclesiastical robes, and there was a passion for bead embroidery in the seventeenth century which corresponds with the enormous expansion of trade to the Far East, Africa and America, perhaps a way of using up the sudden surplus!

Tambour work became fashionable three centuries later, when there was a craze for bead embroidery on bags and belts and even cushions and upholstery. In spite of the development of machinery, dress firms still employ handworkers to make exotic bead fringing and decoration, fashionable in the twenties and now enjoying a new boom in the seventies. Beads were also used in pillow-lace making, to weight the bobbins and make the individual bobbins distinctive.

Small wooden bricks can be drilled for threading, and used for teaching counting and number work as well as manual dexterity. The illustrations show ways of making decorative and effective counting-cards. Each number sheet was made in a different way, then mounted on stiff card and covered with transparent *Fablon* or *Librafilm*. One number, for example, was cut from gay wrapping paper and mounted on a plain ground. Another was cut from magazine print and stuck on a background of brilliant but similar-toned colours, such as patches of different reds torn from a colour supplement. Another was cut from gold paper stuck on dark card, and dark paper could show up well on a bright wallpaper. To be effective and also readable, patterns must be chosen which are fairly uniform in tone. From each card hangs a cord, with some sort of bead or threadable object, in reach for the child to handle and feel as well as see the difference between one, two, three, etc, as true learning involves several senses.

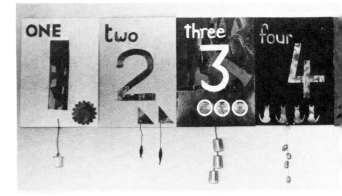

Beads used for teaching counting and number work

Beads used in teaching 'sets'

A home-made abacus can be made with moulded beads. The one overleaf was made with bicycle spokes inserted through a simple wooden frame made to fit them, so that they screw into place. A big box of assorted beads can be used for teaching 'sets' – big and small, dark and light, plain and patterned, striped and spotted, white and coloured, etc. As distinct from pebbles, the results can be strung and labelled for display.

Threading beads

Above left   Ceramic units threaded for decoration

Left   Simple bead abacus

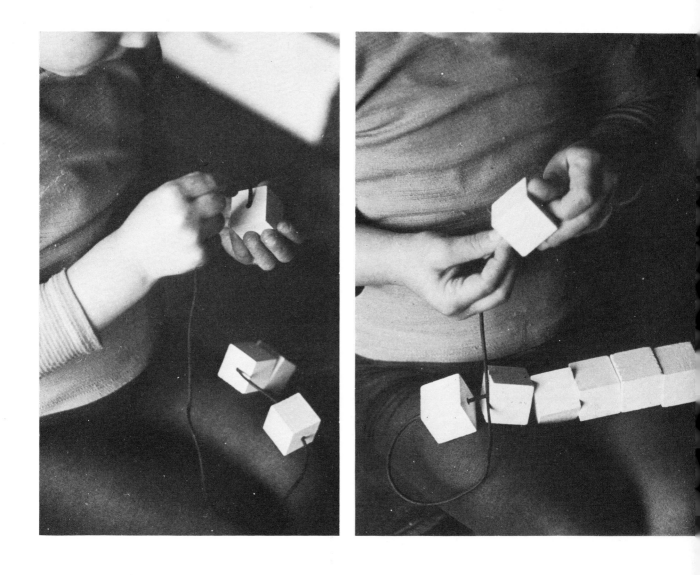

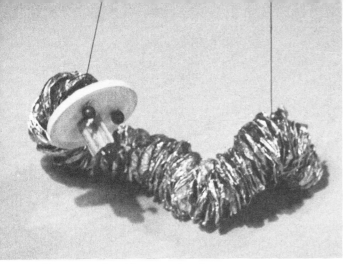

Puppet made with strung bottle tops

Potato puppet

Another form of unit construction which develops logically from stringing beads is toy and puppet-making from units threaded on wire or string. The illustrations show children's toys made from an assortment of inexpensive or collected materials: potatoes, milkbottle tops, plastic tops and cartons, etc. The stoneware dragon was made with units pierced with two parallel holes, to stop twisting, and threaded with thick nylon thread.

This is not a subject where one reaches an end. One idea triggers off another, and craftwise one advances either to more intricate work in glass or precious metals or onto another scale, towards sculpture. Threading beads into necklaces for presents or for dramatic work should be an exercise in aesthetic or artistic choice.

Choosing which to put together is a process which involves sensitivity and patience. It can be very dull to use all beads of the same size, colour and texture, unless they are something very special. It can be equally unsatisfying to have a jumble of all sorts and kinds. On the whole, beads divide into families, as has been shown, but within the families some variety gives interest. A rugged arrangement of bones and wood is enhanced by contrast with coloured round wooden beads partly enclosed in brown acorn cups. Embedded in resin, bones can combine with silver beads in a sophisticated modern setting.

Tiny glass seed beads also combine effectively with natural seed beads, their colour and scale providing a pleasing contrast. This of course is also possible within varieties of seeds. It is worth using nylon or strong linen thread, or even leather thongs for these exercises to be taken seriously. Arranging sea-worn pebbles to balance in colour, shape, tone or texture can be intriguing, and relaxing. Glueing them to leather is a real trial of patience.

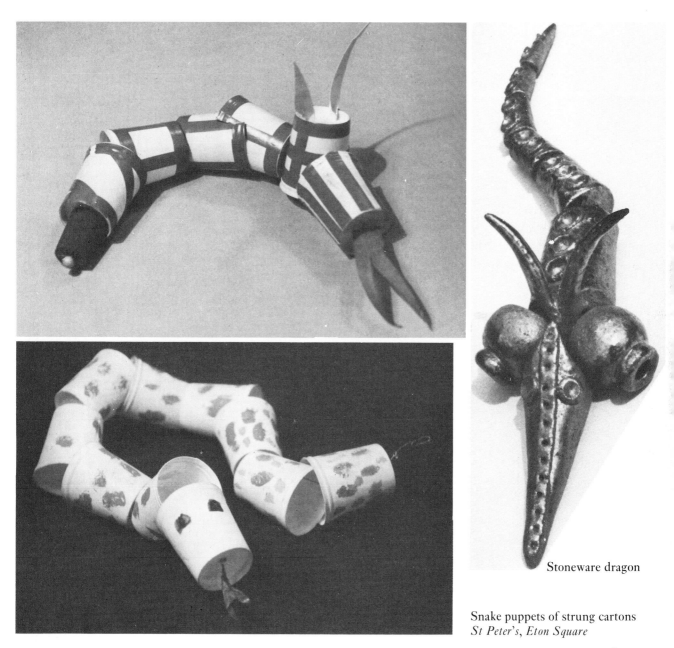

Stoneware dragon

Snake puppets of strung cartons
St Peter's, Eton Square

89

Bead curtain   *Churchill Gardens School*   Seed mosaic set in *Plasticine* (*Plastiline*)

Ceramic constructions and bells
Millchase School, Hampshire

Beads used in dramatic work   *Churchill Gardens School*

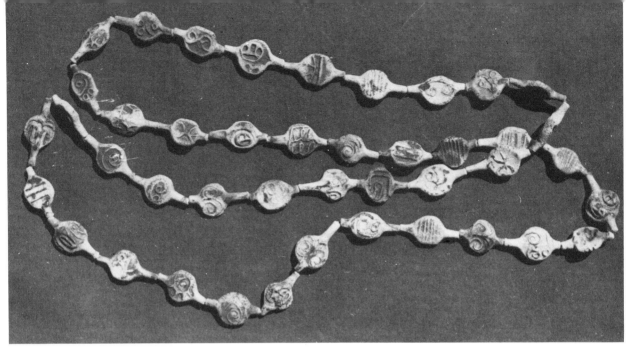

Sawdust-fired burnished clay beads by William Brereton

Necklace of flat beads and leather thongs by William Brereton

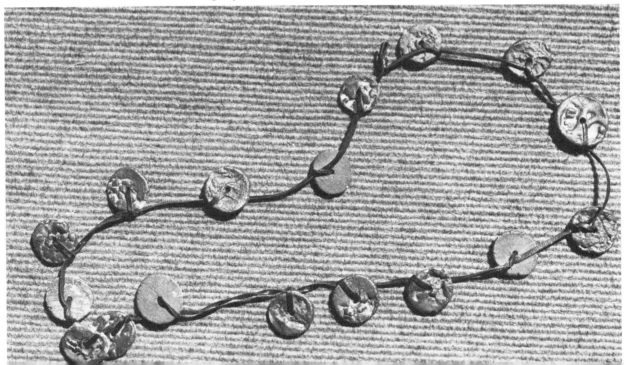

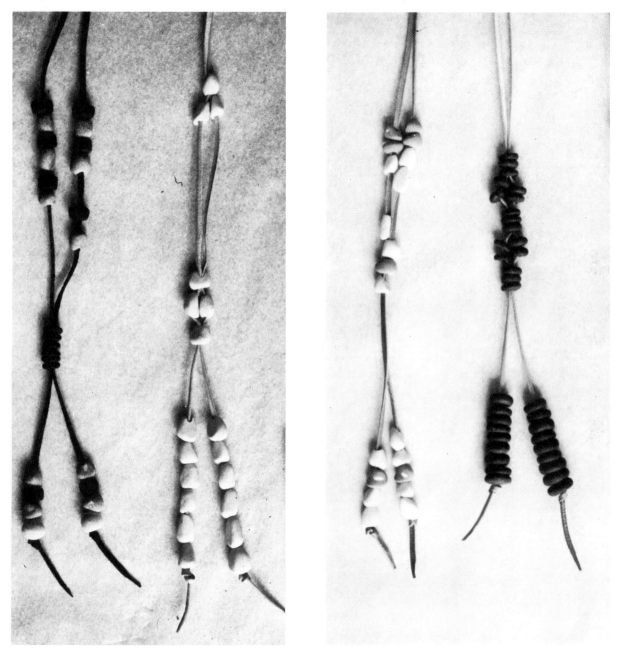

Subtle variations on a theme.   Porcelain and marbled clay beads by Rosemary Brewer

A modern example of bead-weaving accessories by Rachel Forrester

The flow diagram should be both a challenge and warning that the stimulus of the subject could be too wide. A group of students might divide the aspects between them and collectively produce a study of worth without ever exhausting the subject. Children would enjoy the practical work and find it triggers off interest in all manner of things like exploration and travel. Art students could research deeply into processes. The fact that beads in the past have been handled, revered and enjoyed forges a remarkable human link between us and the past. I hope that others will wish to fill in more links of this fascinating chain.

Modern pebble necklace
from the USA
Courtesy Clare Ash

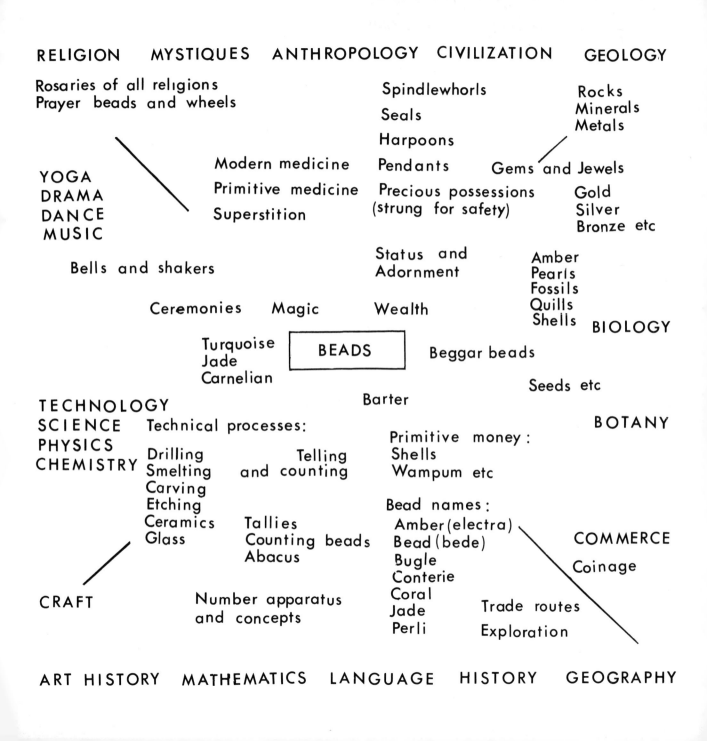

RELIGION   MYSTIQUES   ANTHROPOLOGY   CIVILIZATION   GEOLOGY

Rosaries of all religions
Prayer beads and wheels

Spindlewhorls

Seals

Harpoons

Rocks
Minerals
Metals

YOGA
DRAMA
DANCE
MUSIC

Modern medicine

Primitive medicine

Superstition

Pendants

Precious possessions
(strung for safety)

Gems and Jewels

Gold
Silver
Bronze etc

Bells and shakers

Status and
Adornment

Amber
Pearls
Fossils
Quills
Shells

Ceremonies   Magic   Wealth

BIOLOGY

Turquoise
Jade
Carnelian

BEADS

Beggar beads

Seeds etc

Barter

TECHNOLOGY
SCIENCE
PHYSICS
CHEMISTRY

Technical processes:

Drilling
Smelting
Carving
Etching
Ceramics
Glass

Telling
and counting

Tallies
Counting beads
Abacus

Primitive money:
Shells
Wampum etc

Bead names:
Amber (electra)
Bead (bede)
Bugle
Conterie
Coral
Jade
Perli

BOTANY

COMMERCE

Coinage

CRAFT

Number apparatus
and concepts

Trade routes

Exploration

ART HISTORY   MATHEMATICS   LANGUAGE   HISTORY   GEOGRAPHY

BIBLIOGRAPHY

Bead Embroidery, Joan Edwards, Batsford, London (out of print); Taplinger, New York
The Universal Bead, Joan Mowatt Erikson, Norton, New York
Glass through the Ages, E. Barrington Haynes, Penguin, London
The Story of Money, A. Hingston Quiggin, Methuen, London
The Rose Garden Game, Eithne Wilkins, Herder and Herder, New York
Creating with Beads, Crethe La Croix, Little Craft Series, Sterling Publishing Company, New York; Oak Tree Press, London
History of the Abacus, J. M. Pullan, Hutchinson, London
Hunters and Gatherers, James Woodburn, British Museum
Jewellery from Classical Lands, Reynold Higgins, British Museum.

IN ENCYCLOPEDIAS

See under agate, amber, carnelian, coral, glass, gold, jade, jet, onyx, pearls, turquoise, etc.
Also under beads, jewelry, money, primitive medicine, trade routes, witchdoctors, great explorers and historians.

MUSEUMS TO VISIT

The Ashmolean, Oxford (*Flinders Petrie Collection*)
Beaver House, Great Trinity Lane, London, EC4 (Hudson's Bay Company Headquarters)
British Museum, London WC1
Museum of Mankind (British Museum), Burlington Gardens, London W1
Ethnographical Museum, Cambridge (Beck Collection)
Horniman Museum, Forest Hill, London SE23
London Museum, Kensington Palace , London W8
University College Museum, Gower Street, London WC1

SUPPLIERS

Tools are obtainable from most hardware stores

Papers, clay and adhesives

E J Arnold (School Suppliers)
Butterley Street
Leeds LS10 1AX

also from stationers, art, and hardware stores

Papers of all kinds

Paperchase
216 Tottenham Court Road
London W1

F G Kettle
127 High Holborn
London WC1